THE
Kaleidoscope
BOOK

"Jay-Leido," kaleidoscopic drawing by Betty Tribe

THE *Kaleidoscope* BOOK

A Spectrum of Spectacular Scopes to Make

Sterling Publishing Co., Inc.   New York
A STERLING/LARK BOOK

Edited by
Thom Boswell

Editing: Thom Boswell
Design: Thom Boswell and Sandra Montgomery
Production: Sandra Montgomery, Elaine Thompson,
    Wendy Wells
Photography: Evan Bracken
Drawings: Sandra Montgomery

ISBN 0-8069-8370-1

Library of Congress Cataloging-in-Publication Data

The kaleidoscope book : a spectrum of spectacular scopes to
make / edited by Thom Boswell.
        p.   cm.
    "A Sterling/Lark book."
    Includes bibliographical references (p.   ) and index.
    ISBN 0-8069-8370-1
    1. Kaleidoscope.   1. Boswell, Thom.
QC373.K3K35   1992
688.7'2--dc20   91-38786
                                                       CIP

10 9 8 7 6 5 4 3

A Sterling/Lark Book

First paperback edition published in 1995 by
    Sterling Publishing Company, Inc.
    387 Park Avenue South, New York, N.Y. 10016

Produced by Altamont Press, Inc.
    50 College Street, Asheville, NC 28801

© 1992 by Altamont Press

Distributed in Canada by Sterling Publishing
    % Canadian Manda Group, One Atlantic Avenue, Suite 105
    Toronto, Ontario, Canada M6K 3E7
Distributed in Great Britain and Europe by Cassell PLC
    Wellington House, 125 Strand, London WC2R 0BB, England
Distributed in Australia by Capricorn Link (Australia) Pty Ltd.
    P.O. Box 6651, Baulkham Hills, Business Centre, NSW 2153, Australia

Every effort has been made to ensure that all the information in
this book is accurate. However, due to differing conditions,
tools, and individual skills, the publisher cannot be responsible for any injuries, losses, and other damages which may
result from the use of the information in this book.

Sterling ISBN 0-8069-8370-1 Trade
            0-8069-8371-X Paper

Table of Contents

INTRODUCTION

by Ledell Murphy

Perhaps the magic comes from the perfect blending of art and science in the kaleidoscope, which means an instrument for "viewing beautiful forms." Or perhaps the magic is within each beholder, as we seek beautiful views of the world.

It is exciting for me, as a collector of kaleidoscopes, to share my passion for this magic with you, a potential crafter! My ulterior motive is that, after mastering the basics of kaleidoscope design, you will bring your own talents and imagination to this art form and create new and wonderful scopes for me to add to my collection.

While the primary purpose of this book is to inform you about constructing the physical body of a kaleidoscope, it seems important to balance that information with thoughts about the spirit of the kaleidoscope. After all, kaleidoscopes have to do with symmetry and harmony. So, first we'll take a brief look at the beginnings of the kaleidoscope, as well as the contemporary craze. Then we'll get familiar with the components of a kaleidoscope in a non-technical way, for the purpose of general understanding and vocabulary. We'll also look at some of the ways people view scopes and use them.

Antique reproduction parlor scope by David and Marty Roenigk (opposite).

Stained glass interpretation of a kaleidoscopic image, by Charles Karadimos (right).

HISTORY & CURRENT RENAISSANCE

Sir David Brewster, a Scotsman, first invented the kaleidoscope in 1813, and filed the first patent in 1816. The more I learn about Sir David, the more fitting it seems that he should have developed this wondrous blend of art and science. Sir David was fascinated with science from early childhood, especially with the study of light. His formal education, however, prepared him for the ministry. He was never ordained, but his philosophical beliefs were strongly developed. He was a leading member of the "natural" scientists of the early nineteenth century. One of his tenets was that there need be no conflict between science and religion, and he worked to minimize any such dispute.

Although you may never have heard Sir David's name until now, you are probably familiar with the color wheel. It is Sir David who is credited with identifying red, blue and yellow as the "primary" colors from which all other colors are derived. It was during his experiments with polarized light that he determined this, as well as developed the kaleidoscope.

Sir David earned his living by writing, and by serving as editor of several publications. Although his papers and books, as well as the publications with which he was associated, were scholarly, they were also regarded in a popular vein.

Sir David was not a theorist, but an experimenter. He observed, and tried, and recorded. So as you master the basics of crafting the components of your kaleidoscope, and continue to experiment with variations of the components and with new and different combinations, you can be assured that you are following the approach of the kaleidoscope creator himself.

Kaleidoscopes were instantly successful. Thousands were sold in London and Paris within months, although they were not Sir David's creations. It was called "the great philosophical toy." It seems that from the beginning, people recognized that kaleidoscopes were more than something pretty to look at.

The best known early kaleidoscope maker in America was Charles Green Bush. Prussian by birth, he immigrated to Boston in 1847. His 1873 parlor scope design has been commemorated with reproductions by two contemporary companies. These scopes were often seen in Victorian salons. Bush is best remembered in the kaleidoscope world for "liquid filled ampules." These hand blown tubes were used by Bush as object chamber items, and they created special interest in the images. Only a few contemporary artists have been able to duplicate the process.

More detailed historical information about early kaleidoscope designers, techniques, patents, and uses is available, but is limited. Antique kaleidoscopes, both European and American, are scarce and highly priced.

We all owe a debt of gratitude to the American toy makers, who are principally responsible for keeping kaleidoscopes alive from the early 1900s until the early 1980s. "I haven't seen one of these since I was a kid," is probably the most frequently heard phrase at a showing of contemporary scopes. Many of us recall those childhood memories of kaleidoscopes. And we somehow recapture that childlike sense of wonder and awe once we have occasion to view contemporary kaleidoscopes.

Although there were several kaleidoscope artists on the scene as early as the 1960s and '70s, if there is one person to be credited with

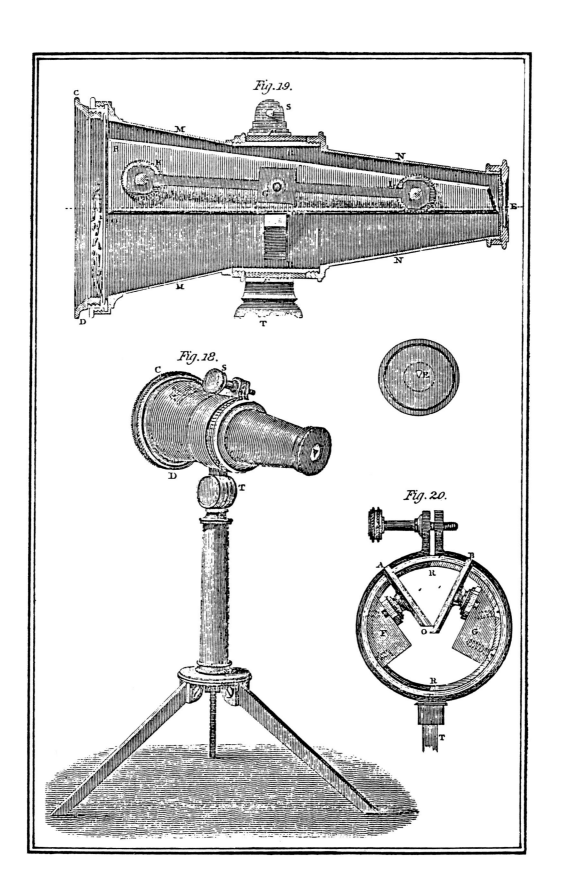

Fig.19.

Fig.18.

Fig.20.

Antique scopes (opposite top), old toy scopes (right) and contemporary scopes (opposite bottom), all from the vast collection of Cozy Baker at Strathmore Hall.

One section of scopes from the collection of Tess & Marty Scherer, the Scherer Gallery (below).

the re-emergence of the kaleidoscope as an important art form, it is Cozy Baker. This warm, energetic, lively, and multi-faceted woman has shared her love for kaleidoscopes with the world. In her 1985 book, *Through the Kaleidoscope*, Cozy introduced us to more than 40 artists then actively making and marketing kaleidoscopes. She also curated the first exhibition of kaleidoscopes in America at Strathmore Hall in suburban Washington, D.C. In 1986, Cozy formed the Brewster Society, gathering together the "designers, collectors, and lovers of kaleidoscopes." The Kaleidoscope Renaissance was underway. The following year, so much had happened in the kaleido-world that Cozy updated her book, issuing it as *Through the Kaleidoscope… And Beyond*. Nearly 100 artists were featured. In 1990, Cozy gave us *KALEIDORAMA*, a fun and fanciful book. There has been a calendar, many articles in periodicals, national news features, philanthropic donations of scopes, gallery shows, museum exhibits, national conventions, and regional gatherings—all because this woman took her talents and know-how, combined them with her passion for kaleidoscopes, brought together kindred spirits, and shared these wonderful "philosophical toys" as they re-emerged in the art world. The kaleido-community that Cozy has fostered has a synergy as wonderful as kaleidoscopes themselves. By encouraging new artists and promoting the highest quality scopes with collectors and galleries, the art form has blossomed and grown. And the spirits of many participants have been individually nurtured while melding into a living kaleidoscope.

One factor that new kaleidoscope makers should be aware of is the high ethical standards that knit the kaleido-community together. Most of the kaleidoscopes you see in books, articles, galleries and shows are copyrighted or patented. There is important legal and moral respect for the "ownership" of the concepts that have been developed. This ethical concern is shared by collectors and gallery owners as well.

The number of artists, and collectors, continuously increases, and the variety of wonderful scopes now available is astonishing. But at any gathering of kaleido-crazies, ideas are generated for more scopes than anyone has yet had time to produce. There is a place for you.

COMPONENTS

Sir David wrote that not one in a thousand makers, nor one in ten thousand viewers, of kaleidoscopes would know or understand the optical principles on which they are based. He seemed to want us to enjoy them anyway, so this non-technical description of the components may be enough for most of you. However, more technical information appears later in the book, and those of you who want to learn the physics may be even more creative in the designs of your own scopes.

Although there are generally four basic components of a kaleidoscope (eye piece, external presentation, mirror system, and object chamber), there are many variations of each of these components—and new variations waiting to be implemented by you. The variations of these individual components, along with a few other design considerations (such as objects in the chamber and light source), can be combined in limitless ways to create new and wonderful scopes.

The Kaleidoscopic Image

It's often difficult to know where to begin, but in this case it seems obvious to begin at the end. It is impossible to discuss the various components without first discussing the goal.

"Krystoscope," kaleidoscopic art (originally in color) rendered by **Betty Tribe.**

Two-mirror images, by Charles Karadimos

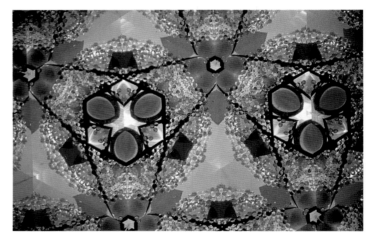

Three-mirror images, by Carolyn Bennett

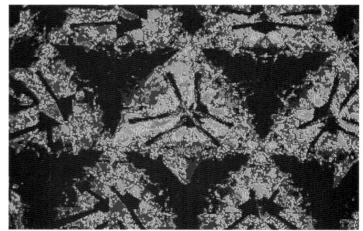

Computer generated images, by Karl Schilling

"Irribundance 40," kaleidoscopic drawing by Betty Tribe, commissioned by the Irrigation Association (courtesy of Hunter Industries).

In each decision you make about how you want to vary the mirror system, or object chamber, or objects, or even in how you want to present your scope, the ultimate goal is to produce wondrous images. After all, Brewster chose the name "kaleidoscope" to describe an instrument for viewing beautiful forms. While the presentation may be wondrous to behold, and sculptural art in itself, what makes it a kaleidoscope is its beautiful images.

You have seen examples of kaleidoscope images in some quilt patterns, in snowflakes, in tie-dyeing patterns, and in fireworks displays. There are two common images. (See photos on page 14.) One is a "mandala": a circular, snowflake-like pattern that appears at the end of the barrel. The other type fills your entire field of vision. Both are comprised of three-sided replications of the objects in the object chamber. Both have rhythm and harmony and intricacies. Each has visual integrity and impact.

People often have preferences for one or the other. Many kaleidoscope artists make scopes that produce both types of image. There are even artists that combine two different mirror systems in the same kaleidoscope so that you can look at either image type. And there are other mirror designs which produce further variations of image patterns.

There is special magic in a kaleidoscopic image. The colors, shapes, forms, and patterns combine in ever-changing, seldom-repeating relationships. The kaleidoscopic mandala has been called a metaphor for the New Age. The image can be thought of as the world, with diversity in its pieces, but unification when viewed in its totality. The image can be thought of as life, filled with unexpected beauty to be enjoyed. And just as Nature is filled with symmetry and balance, so are the images created by you in your kaleidoscope.

External Presentation

The simplest way to think of the external presentation is how the kaleidoscope might look displayed on a coffee table. Although the other components could conceivably be held together with masking tape, and still have the most beautiful images imaginable, they wouldn't be very attractive from the outside. So a pleasing exterior becomes important.

Your childhood memory of a kaleidoscope may be of a cardboard tube, 6 to 8 inches in length, and 1 to 3 inches in diameter. The tube you remember may have been covered in colorful paper, perhaps with a theme. Toy makers and contemporary scope artists still offer wonderful pieces in cardboard tubes.

But it is in the external presentation that the most obvious variety occurs. In general, scope makers bring their previous artistic talents and skills to the presentation of their scopes. For example, stained glass artists who begin making scopes might offer a stained glass housing, using wonderful colors, patterns and textures of glass to make the piece beautiful to look at from the outside. Woodworkers may offer a lathe-turned barrel, perhaps with inlay. Metalworkers might use hammered brass or silver, decorated with an enameled design. A whimsical sense of humor can also be exercised by creating scopes with presentations that are pure fun.

External presentations can sometimes be of equal importance to the images inside. Some scopes are offered in fantasy settings, complete with flowing water and sparkling external lights. Some are offered in large abstract architectural shapes. One scope maker has joined with a sculptor to incorporate a scope into cast figures of very large scale. Another designer, who raises prize poultry, uses goose eggs for her presentation.

Whatever talents and skills and interests you already have can be used to create your own exterior. I have yet to see stiffened crochet, bread dough sculpture, embroidery, basketry, quilting, scrimshaw, or corn husks used as exteriors. Your own kaleidoscope's design is an opportunity to re-apply your current passions to another art form.

There are a few considerations in the external presentations. Is your scope to be a parlor scope or handheld? A parlor scope usually sits at an angle on an arm attached to a

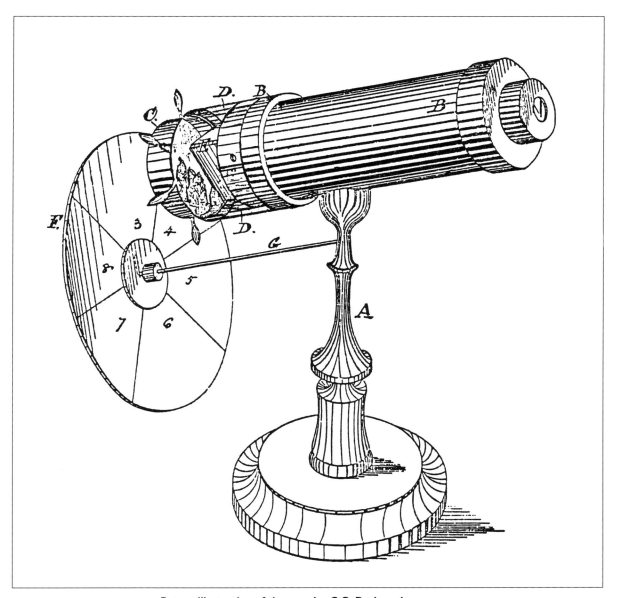

Patent illustration of the popular C.G. Bush parlor scope.

base. It can be viewed without lifting it. This would be important for very heavy or very large scopes. Occasionally the scope itself is detachable for use as a handheld scope. Often a handheld is accompanied by some (usually small) stand to use for displaying it—and to keep it from rolling off the table.

Another consideration is size. Lengths and diameters range from 1-inch miniatures to the world's largest, over 12 feet. You may want your scope to be wearable. Some artists offer scopes as fine pieces of jewelry—pendants for a chain, tie tacks, bracelets, and rings.

Often there is some coordination of the exterior presentation with the images created inside. This coordination may be in the color scheme used, thematic motifs, or in the general "feel" of the scope.

Your chosen mirror system and object chamber may dictate some size and shape parameters for the external presentation. Or you may know how you want the exterior to look, thereby placing some limitations on the other components. It's one of those "which came first, the chicken or the egg," questions. And there is no rule.

As you perfect your kaleidoscope construction skills and critique your own work, or as you look at kaleidoscopes in galleries and shops, you may want to consider evaluating the external presentation in terms of workmanship. In selecting a new scope for my collection, it is important to me that the workmanship be of the highest quality. Attractive and pleasing appearance are matters of personal choice, of course. Another of my considerations is how comfortable the scope is to hold and view for extended periods of time.

Mirror Systems

It is the mirror system of a kaleidoscope that creates the magic. The mirror shape, the number of mirrors used, and the angle(s) at which the mirrors are joined combine to produce the pattern of image you see. The toy scopes we remember were generally made with highly polished metal, not glass mirrors, in a straight shape, two-mirror, 60° angle system. This produces a mandala: a single, symmetrical, circular "snowflake" at the end of the tube. The other most popular system is three straight mirrors in an equilateral triangle. This system produces a faceted pattern that fills the entire field of view.

There are other variations using four or more mirrors, tapering the mirrors, and circular systems using flexible, reflective materials. Some artists are making poly-angular mirror systems. That is, there is a mechanism that allows the two-mirror system's angle to be altered. Other variations include altering the angle(s) at which the mirrors are placed. Narrower angles increase the number of replications, which, in general, add to the complexity of the image. There is opportunity with the mirror system for much experimentation.

When I evaluate a kaleidoscope, I look closely at the mirror system. Dust particles or fingerprints are not acceptable. And I look for a mirror system that is sealed to prevent dust and dirt from entering it. Quality kaleidoscopes are made with first- (or front-) surface mirrors. These have the reflective coating on the top surface of the glass rather than behind the glass, as is the case with most common mirrors. First-surface mirrors give a sharper, truer image. They are also more expensive. An invisible seam where the mirrors join is difficult to accomplish, but is an indication of highest quality workmanship. I also evaluate the mirror system implementation by looking closely at the image. The mirror system should create regularity in the pattern replication. The symmetry should be perfect, or near perfect, with certain angles, and have no distracting diversion along the pattern lines.

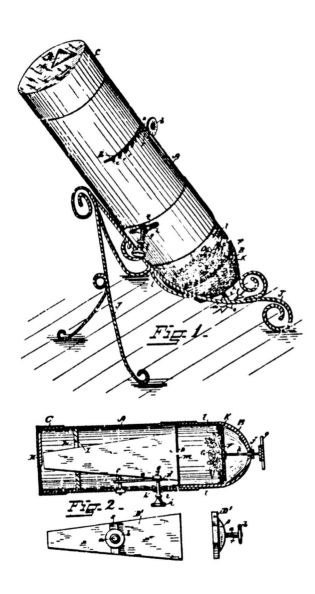

Drawing of kaleidoscope patented by R. Leach, 1885.

Object Chamber

The object chamber is also referred to as the "cell." It is the object chamber that holds the objects you choose to replicate with your mirror system. Some scopes have no object chamber and no objects. These are called teleidoscopes. They could be open-ended but often have some sort of lens at the end. The world becomes your object chamber, since whatever the scope is pointed at becomes replicated. This is truly a different way of viewing the world.

The most basic chamber is fixed inside the last inch or so of the barrel. You view a scope with this type of object chamber by rotating the entire barrel. Another type of object chamber turns independently while the barrel is held in a fixed position. As the barrel or cell is turned, the objects tumble, and the image changes.

Yet another type of object chamber is the "wheel." Objects are incorporated into a relatively flat circle, usually larger than the barrel of the scope. The wheel is attached to the end of the barrel, and rotates independently. Naturally, wheels don't have to be flat. There are other quite fanciful shapes that are used as wheels. One very popular variation of the wheel (so popular, in fact, that it is generally given its own category) is the marble. A marble is attached to the end of the barrel, and is turned to produce different images. Some marbles are hand blown, some especially for kaleidoscopes. They can be quite dramatic, and are usually interchangeable. For interchangeable object chambers, wheels and marbles seem to be less complicated to engineer.

Interchangeable object chambers offer a lot of variety. With a single mirror system and presentation, the viewer gets multiple kaleidoscopes by changing the object chamber.

The objects in a chamber may be freely tumbling in air, or suspended in oil. An oil-filled chamber causes slower motion of the objects, and the motion continues after you have stopped rotating the scope.

Some object chambers are designed to be opened. Into these chambers, the viewer can insert different objects. These are quite effective for getting new views of common items.

When critiquing your object chamber, you will want to be sure that the turning is smooth, oil doesn't leak, and that all joinings are secure and appear "finished."

Objects

By now you know that objects can be contained within an object chamber or imbedded in a wheel. Objects considered most appropriate are colorful, small, textural, and translucent. These might be plastic or glass beads and chips, seeds, crystals, marbles, string…the list is endless. Textured, colorful glass is often used for wheels. Wildflowers and butterfly wings are examples of objects that are effective when cast in plastic wheels or sandwiched between clear panes. There are even scopes that use 35mm color slides as a wheel.

Messages, such as Happy Birthday, I Love You, and Get Well Soon, are sometimes used as objects. One of the most creative was a marriage proposal. You might think of coordinating a scope's message with its exterior to celebrate a special occasion.

Combining colors and shapes and sizes of objects is a personal and challenging process. It takes much experimentation to collect the objects that produce spectacular images. When I am looking at a scope, I am rarely aware of the particular pieces being used in the object chamber. What I do look for is constant surprise in the images, which, in general, means that the objects can move freely. I am wary of seemingly unintentional broken pieces, or pieces that stick in corners of the cell.

Variations

Some artists have mastered Brewster's polarized light scopes. Clear, flat objects are placed between polarized light filters for spectacular images with wonderful coloration. Sometimes the objects themselves are polarized. There are also scopes that use fluids of different colors. The colors don't mix with each other, and the replication of their swirling produces a delightful image. There is a sound-activated scope. A microphone in the circuitry activates the various shapes and colors. There are uses for fiber optics in scopes. A special variation is the projection scope. The images are rear-screen or forward-projected in varying sizes. (I am still waiting for a projection scope that I can afford.)

And for high-tech lovers, there is computer software that creates beautiful images. One program in the public domain is based on random generation, so the images are never repeated, and you can alter the speed at which the images change.

Other Considerations

In addition to the major components of exterior presentation, mirror system and object chamber, there are a few other factors to be aware of. The eyepiece, for example, is typically a round hole in a covering of the viewing end of the barrel. This hole is generally centered in respect to the mirror system. However, there are variations in shape, size and placement. The eyepiece may be a pointed oval or eye-shaped, or may be the full size and shape of the end of the mirror system. There are some binocular eyepieces. Some viewing holes are offset from the mirror system center, giving unusual views of the image.

To be sure your images are as clear as possible, you may want to use an optical lens in the eyepiece. Keeping in mind that the human eye (normal vision) has a minimum focal length of 6 to 8 inches, you may notice image distortion if your scope's length differs significantly. Optical lenses can also provide magnification of the image for even more impressive viewing. Lenses are either glass or plastic, and can be cut to fit your eyepiece. There are even collectors who have had special glasses or eyepiece attachments prepared for them to aid in viewing.

Another important consideration is the light source. Generally, you will have a transparent or translucent covering at the end of your object chamber, and the light will enter through that end of the scope. Some object chambers are designed to be side-lighted; that is, an opaque end piece is used for the object chamber, and the sides of the object chamber are translucent. Some kaleidoscopes are presented with internal light sources, or lights built into the stand of a parlor scope.

Whatever design technique you use, you must always be aware of how and where and how much light will enter your scope. After all, it is the reflection of light that produces an effective image.

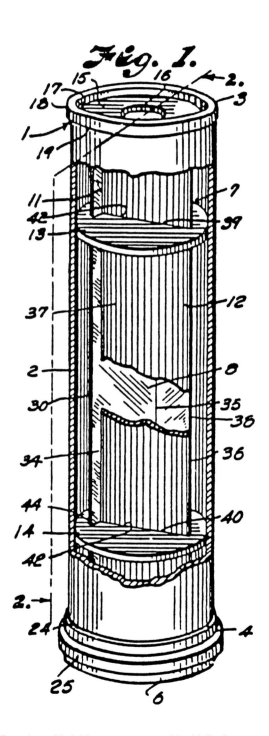

Drawing of kaleidoscope patented by H. B. Grow, 1961.

VIEWING

After investing the time to design and construct your kaleidoscope, you can spend the rest of your life enjoying it, and sharing it. Many kaleidoscope enthusiasts have had the experience of sharing a scope with someone who looks through it briefly, returns it, and says "you must see something in there that I don't." I think that must be true. Like most visual art, kaleidoscopic images are personal and interactive. The viewer brings his/her persona to the experience—and not everyone is willing or able to be so exposed.

There are different settings and techniques for enjoying your kaleidoscopes. While the usual technique is to aim the scope upward at a bright light, some scopes are more effective, or give a different experience, if viewed in the dark. You can use a lamp for a light source, but also try a focused beam from a small flashlight. Move the flashlight around to different angles and spots of light. Candlelight can also be an effective light source for some scopes. Effects produced with fluorescent and incandescent light are also interesting. Of course, many scopes are particularly dramatic in bright sunlight. Also, simply tapping the barrel is sometimes more effective than rotating it. Varying the speed at which you turn the object chamber produces different viewing experiences. In fact, some members of the kaleido-community are known as either "fast turners" or "slow turners."

Kaleidoscopic viewing makes great party entertainment. One couple who received a scope for a wedding gift reportedly had to remind guests that they were there to visit, not to look at scopes. It is certainly fun to "ooh and aah," and try to pass an especially wonderful image intact to a friend. On the other hand, solitary viewing offers a rich, internally satisfying experience.

It seems that I am able to get whatever I need at the moment from a viewing experience. It is the nature of a scope that it can be either stimulating or soothing. By focusing on the intricacies of the pattern, I feel excitement. Or by concentrating on the totality, the symmetry, I feel calmed.

To enable myself to explore creative solutions to vocational or personal problems, I use kaleidoscope viewing to keep my mind open, to look for different alternatives. Many professional people report keeping a few scopes in the office for just that exercise. I also find that kaleidoscope viewing is a healthy way of relaxing and coping with stress. I see beauty and wholeness, and a reminder that there is harmony in all of life's changes.

Therapists are using the kaleidoscope as a metaphor to help clients understand life cycles. They are also recommended for helping in the search for balance of body, mind and spirit. Health organizations have found kaleidoscopes helpful in accomplishing some of their goals. The Hospice organization has used scopes with both dying patients and family members. Children's hospitals use scopes with patients undergoing long treatment. Holding and turning scopes and getting such immediate reward in beautiful images is also good therapy for people who need to exercise their hands. Kaleidoscopes are particularly effective in enhancing meditation. It seems to me that all kaleidoscope viewing is a form of meditation, even unconsciously. Perhaps it is a joyful and fun experience, but at the same time we are gaining a renewal of spirit. We get the benefit of color and harmony in every viewing, whether it is purposeful concentration or not.

While I participated for years in what I skeptically called "recreational growth experiences," I could not understand the talk about "centering" yourself. I had no idea what this meant, and had no clue how to accomplish it. Finally, viewing a mandala image, I could understand. Over time I have been able to internalize the balance, harmony, and wholeness of the images into my own mind and spirit. This didn't happen immediately. For the first year or so, I just knew that I found scopes relaxing and peaceful, and better than a glass of wine for getting to sleep at night. I even felt an unexplained and warm kinship with the scope artists and collectors that I met. Now I have come to feel there must be some exchange of "soul" that occurs when I view a scope, even by an artist I have never met.

So as you are creating your kaleidoscopes, and putting some of your soul into them, know that you are communicating with those who will view your scopes. They may appreciate your craftsmanship, but in seeing the images you've created, they may also glimpse the beauty in your soul. This is truly a wonderful gift.

CONTEMPORARY GALLERY

Dan Sudnick

This one-of-a-kind kaleidoscope, entitled "Vocation-Avocation," is a combination of my vocational skills as a plumber and the reflection of my mind's eye. It began 20 years ago as a project at a trade school open-house to demonstrate the joining of copper pipe and fittings, and has continued to evolve. I admit that it may never be finished, as I continue to add old or unusual fittings from time to time. My interest in kaleidoscopes was inspired by my wife, a very creative mechanical engineer. She started making kaleidoscopes from stained glass years ago.

The lamp-scope shown here has three kaleidoscopes mounted in various positions. Each scope can be removed for individual viewing. One scope has an object case filled with oil. The second scope has three hand-blown glass marbles, and the third scope has four interchangeable object cases. Each object case or marble is displayed in a unique fashion under each scope. I have since created another series of intricate plumbing scopes entitled "Copper Madness."

"Vocation-Avocation" lamp stand incorporates five handmade scopes, each with interchangeable marbles and object chambers.

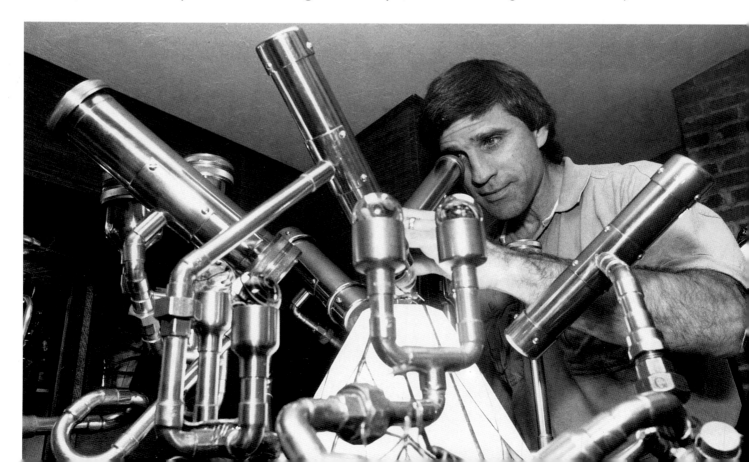

Willie Stevenson

My approach to making scopes is that of a sculptor, creating signed and numbered limited editions, of which "Home Planet #1" and "Outbound: An In-Viro-Mental Statement" (a 1991 Niche Award winner) are examples. I also do one-of-a-kinds and am available for commissioned work with special emphasis on coin operation and kinetics.

My most notable piece to date is a winner of the Brewster Society Award For Creative Ingenuity titled "Whatever Blows Your Skirt Up," now residing in the home/museum of Cozy Baker and renamed by her, "Whatever Tilts Your Kilts." It's a 6' L. x 6' H. x 3' W., motorized, poly-angular scope with hand-painted silks revolving above a fan at the object-end of the 12" x 48" first surface mirrors. Stereo speakers at the eyepiece provide continuous music. At the flip of the switch the mirrors start opening and closing, and the stunning, randomly formed image dances seductively in perfect beat to whatever music is playing. The matching of the audio and visual elements is what I call "cerebrally synchro-nized," and the total experi-ence is a kaleidoscopic mas-sage for the soul.

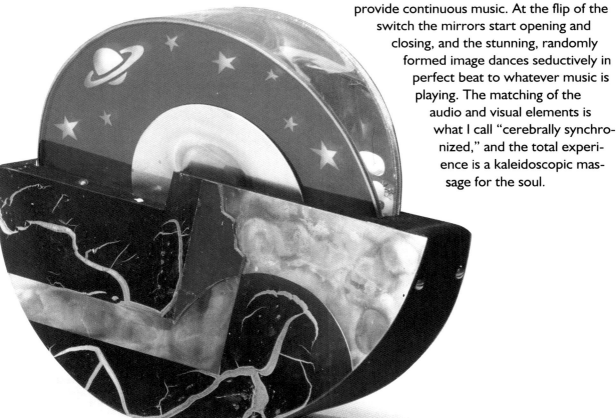

"Outbound: An In-Viro-Mental Statement" (above).

"Home Planet #1" (below).

Steven Gray

As of late, kaleidoscopes have offered a wonderful mixture of optics, woodwork, gadgetry and a freedom of design which fits my personality very well. Kaleidoscopes have such a fascination and mystique that to do them justice, I feel that the outside appearance should have an attraction making it hard for most people to pass them by without stopping to investigate further. Although kaleidoscopes go back to the early 1800s, there are no prescribed limits on artistic interpreta-

Interior view of parasol pattern (left).

tions. My current designs have no traditional counterparts, although my interpretation might remind one of old world navigating devices.

Another important aspect to me is the selection of wood and the effect that it will have on the overall feeling of the kaleidoscope. Since I use some exceptionally figured woods, it is very important that I use the wood to its fullest potential. Only then have I done the wood justice. My reward is the satisfaction and enjoyment of a wonderful piece of wood fashioned into an object of an equally pleasing nature.

Stephen and Carmen Gallo Colley

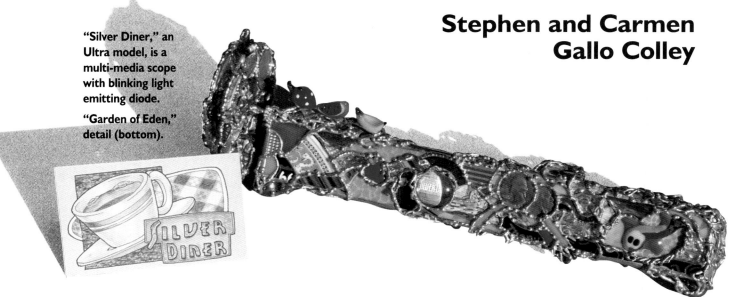

"Silver Diner," an Ultra model, is a multi-media scope with blinking light emitting diode.

"Garden of Eden," detail (bottom).

In 1978, we were stained glass panel designers and joined an artist co-op gallery in downtown San Antonio. Most customers were tourists looking for small gifts which travel well in suitcases. Producing such an item was the inspiration for the first Gallocolley kaleidoscope.

Thirteen years and hundreds of kaleidoscopes later, the table top and jewelry kaleidoscopes we produce bear little resemblance to our first ones. Working on the theory that there is no such thing as too much embellishment, and driven by the feeling that each scope should look better than the one made before it, Gallocolley Opdesign table scopes include just about any kind of material which can withstand the heat of assembly. The Ultra model scopes, each with a unique name, design and theme, can include as many as 400 individual parts and often take over 120 hours to produce.

Carmen relies on her jewelry construction background to make her necklace scopes. These tiny scopes incorporate precious and semi-precious jewels, stones and heat-treated glass particles to provide an easy way to take the colorful and soothing kaleidoscopic images everywhere.

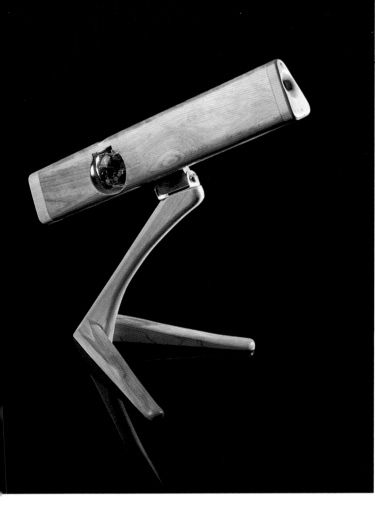

Henry Bergeson

I started out as a mechanical engineer working on projects ranging from the development of modern sailing rigs for cargo ships, to boat building and medical instrument design. While certain aspects of this work were always interesting, I felt there was something lacking in terms of creative freedom. When a downturn in business found me out of a job, I had some freedom to explore other directions. That freedom led to a happy entanglement in the world of kaleidoscopes. My focus in this world has been to gather up bits of my past experiences and knowledge to create unique, interactive kaleidoscopes with extraordinary images and rugged construction.

"Luna Scope" (left) is a 2-mirror parlor scope that is detachable. It features a hand-blown glass object chamber with its own rechargeable light source. "Treasure Chest" (below) is a versatile scope available in 2- or 3-mirror format with interchangeable objects. Photos by Michael Fulks.

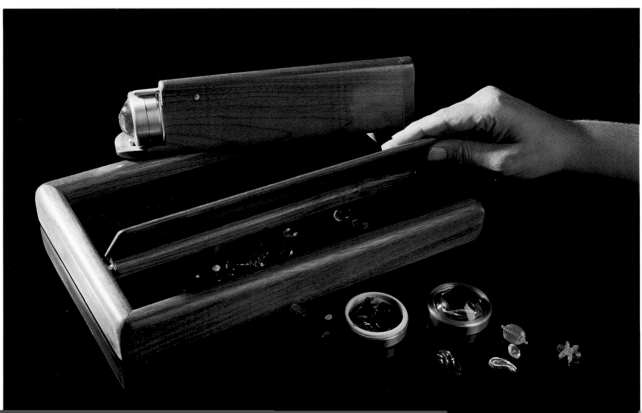

David Kalish

The kaleidoscope is a wonderful optical instrument that creates order out of chaos, providing us with a sense of symmetry, balance, and harmony. These are elements which I attempt to carry over into the exterior designs of each of my works.

Special emphasis is given to the interior optical components of my kaleidoscopes. The object cases contain pieces suspended in pure mineral oil. Mostly natural objects are used. Pieces are carefully selected and combined to produce optimum imaging. Lighting is an essential ingredient. My designs utilize variable front and side lighting with different backgrounds and translucencies.

"Melting Moments" (above) features an unusual oil-filled object chamber. Photo by Douglas Campbell.

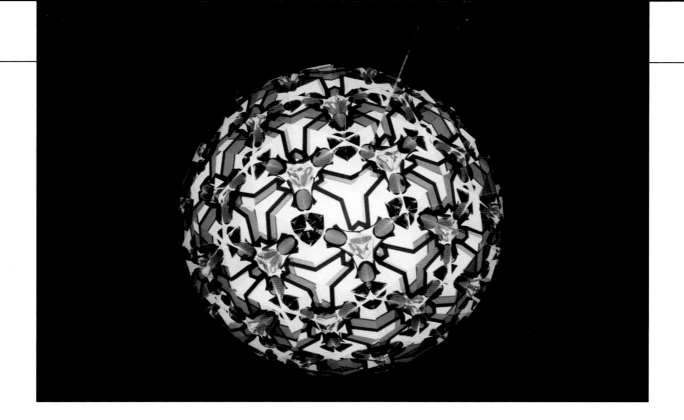

My wood pieces have been created in collaboration with fellow craftsman Thomas Crothers. We use a variety of exotic hardwoods. The brass pieces are made of solid brass, buffed to a mirror finish.

My creations are both sculptural and architectural with a distinctively modern, contemporary look.

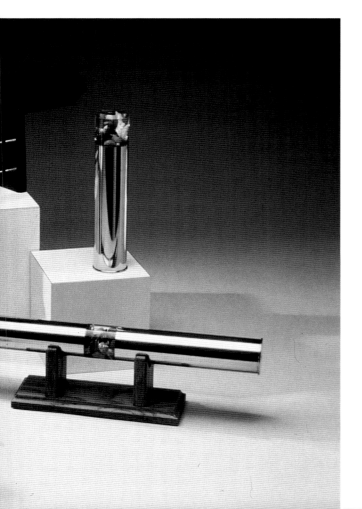

Interior (top), photo by Douglas Campbell.

An array of designs (left) including, clockwise from left: "Odyssey," "Sea Fantasy - I," "The Wedding - I," "Sea Fantasy - II," "The Wedding - II," and "Classical Brass." Photo by Ron Didinato.

Dean Krause

When I was about eight years old, I dismantled my first kaleidoscope. Twenty-one years later I built my first, for a friend. Eventually, I began selling them, and giving them as gifts. Kaleidoscopes are, to me, a very unique art form. Part machine, part divine, they unite the human qualities that are usually separate. They illustrate that order can come out of chaos. The viewer has a sense of involvement, being able to change their view of the world at will.

I have many reasons to build kaleidoscopes, but by far, expressing my own creativity is the most important. I feel that artists change the state of consciousness they

experience, then create something that has that energy ingrained into it. If others are open to the experience, they can use that art as a bridge, to become a different person.

"Kaleido-Ring," top, and "Beautiful," bottom (photo above) feature dichroic glass objects with 2-mirror systems. Photo by Mark Wenzel.

Four scopes (left), clockwise from front left: Kaleido-8"; "Pillars of the Universe," an organic parlor scope with 4-mirror system; "Uxmal," with turning quartz crystal and green marble slab; "Captain Nemo's Personal Ray Machine," a battery-powered kaleido projector with changeable object cells. Photo by Eric Lovejoy.

Audrey Barna

When I was a child, my father raised poultry. My mother once attended a lecture on egg art, where it was mentioned that goose eggs were very much in demand among egg artists. Through this contact, I met someone who introduced me to the world of egging.

I believe I am the first person to make a kaleidoscope egg. I wanted to make something different, something I had never seen done before with an egg. I had always loved kaleidoscopes, but don't know exactly what triggered the connection.

Egg art has been the most fulfilling thing I have ever done in my life. It provides an income, friends, travel, business experience, an outlet for creativity, respect of my peers, and self esteem. Also, the geese, ducks and chickens are earning their keep!

Goose egg scopes with front-turning 2-mirror systems. Photo by Tess Scherer.

Charles Karadimos

As a self-taught glass artist since 1976 and kaleidoscope maker since 1979, dealing with light and color have been a primary concern. The kaleidoscope fulfills this, not just because it is a colorful toy, but because it enables one to respond immediately to various combinations of color, shape, and light with the simple turning of an object case.

All of my scopes are handcrafted entirely of glass, with individuality and quality being of utmost importance. The exteriors are constructed using fusing and slumping techniques, with the focus on a clean look and a balanced feel. However, the imagery produced by the scope I feel is the most important aspect. All of the glass in the free-moving object case is selected to

coordinate with the exterior glass. Since it is imperative that color balance and random imagery be maintained, each piece is carefully shaped, lamp-worked, melted, fused, and/or cut. This, in combination with a variety of mirror systems, results in patterns that are very intricate, attention-holding and emotion-provoking.

"Obelisk," with battery-powered interior lights (opposite top).

"Fused/Slumped Set" with interchangeable object cases (opposite bottom).

Interior image with six-point symmetry (top left).

"Cone" and **"Parlor Cone,"** made of slumped glass (top right).

"Delta II" binocular, with 3-D image (left).

Douglas Johnson

The new kaleidoscope designs I have created (marble scope, satellite scopes, scopeitall, binocular scope and the carousel) have emerged because of a playful attitude, a willingness to explore, and a fascination with the questions, "I wonder how it will look if…" and "How can the kaleidoscope experience be improved?"

As one of the early pioneers of this particular kaleidoscope renaissance, I emerged through the stained glass world. Windseye kaleidoscopes reflect this origin as well as an earlier fascination with 19th century brass instrument technology. My work has been described by others as typifying the "Jules Verne" era.

Kaleidoscopes have been for me the greatest possible playground of opportunities! Through kaleidoscopic creation, invention, design, and production I have been able to realize almost all of my childhood and adult dreams.

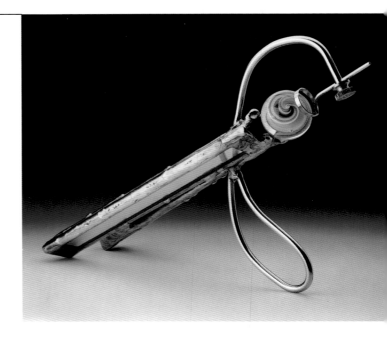

"Windseye Marble Binocular Kaleidoscope" (above). Photo by Chuck Johnson.

"Carousel," "Light Vein," "Crystoscope," and "Rolascope," from top (below). Photo by Ralph Grabriner.

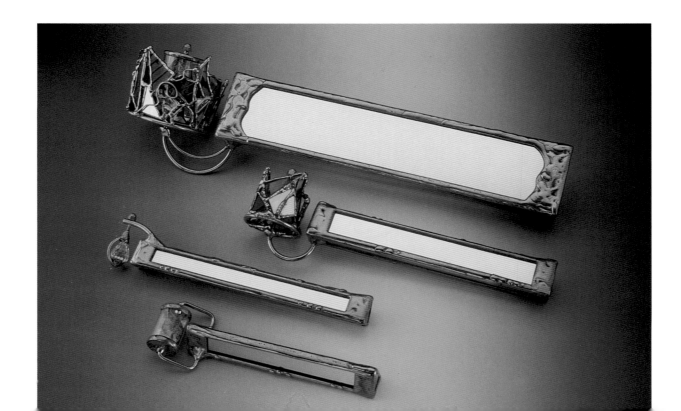

Don Doak

When making a kaleidoscope, my goal is to create a quality scope that, 100 years from today, an antique collector will be able to spot from across the room and immediately identify as a "Don Doak kaleidoscope." By applying all the skills, crafts, and trades I have worked at in my life, I feel I may be able to achieve this goal.

I design and build many of my tools, ranging from a special glass cutter to cut my mirror, to building a large kiln capable of rapidly bending, fusing and/or irridizing glass in an airtight, controlled environment.

Each kaleidoscope is made completely by me. My scopes are labor-intensive, and the design I have developed is unique, as it came from within me. From the beginning, I have felt that, rather than coming up with a new design every few months, I would strive to improve and perfect the design I have. My hope is that by combining precision in shape, form, function, quality material and workmanship, I will someday produce the perfect kaleidoscope.

Two "Liquid Wheel" kaleidoscopes (below) with two "Musical Geodyssey" scopes and accessory box, all made of irridized glass. Photo by Schepp.

David and Marty Roenigk

Sir David's Reflections was started by brothers David and Marty Roenigk due to the demand for antique kaleidoscopes. We started out by collecting antique scopes and selling extras. When the demand got too great, we decided to produce exact reproductions using the same materials, paying particular attention to size, weight and mirror systems. But because we believe that the objects in the object case are the heart and soul of the kaleidoscope, we faithfully reproduced the same glass and designs that the original artists intended for each scope. We also employed Steve Auger to design new objects for a new look in the old scopes.

"The Queen Anne" (above) features a changeable object case and collapses to 3 inches.

Object case (right) from "The Victoria II."

"The Victoria II" (opposite) is a brass and mahogany parlorscope containing precious and semi-precious stones as well as detailed lampwork ampules in its object case.

Shantidevi

My work, life work, art work, inner and outer work is about healing. It's about bringing some light, laughter and natural order into a world that has lost its connection to a natural sense of the divine. Kaleidoscopes have always been a mystical vehicle for me. The ever changing gifts within transport me to that place in the heart of silence that nourishes my spirit and sustains my courage in these tumultuous times. The spheres I've made are also spiritual for me. Even their form is synonymous with wholeness. I experience a deep peacefulness holding and viewing them. It is my hope that my work will move others for a moment to that place that is bigger than all of us and contains all of our differences in grace and beauty, a reminder of our unity with all.

Group of kaleidoscopes and spheres (above).

"Let the Dreamers Wake the Nation" (right), by Shantidevi and Sugito, with spheres and object chamber containing liquid filled ampules.

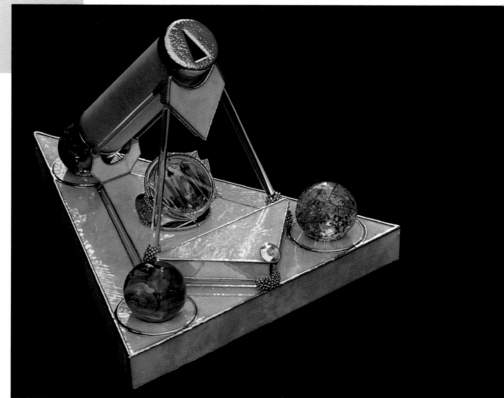

Dorothy Marshall

When I made my first kaleidoscope in 1971, I didn't realize I would be poor as a churchmouse and living in an unheated attic while I struggled to break through the prevailing notion of kaleidoscopes as "just a dimestore toy." After hundreds of discouraging rejections from fair directors and gallery owners, perseverance paid off and my handmade kaleidoscopes were accepted into the top arts and crafts shows in the country where they won various awards. Favorable reviews in the New York Times and other media followed.

Luckily, about this time I fell in love with Ethan Allen, a scientist. Together we drafted a proposal for an exhibit which integrated the art and science of kaleidoscopes. I became the creative director of this exhibit, *Kaleidoscopes: Reflections of Science and Art,* which was toured nationally for three years by the Smithsonian with primary funding from the National Science Foundation. It firmly established kaleidoscopes' newly won credibility with millions of museum visitors. At Harvard, other universities, and the

"Chinese Landscape" by Dorothy Marshall and Indra Stern, made of flame-tempered handcarved bamboo. Photo by Carol Westlake.

Smithsonian, our classes sold out and received rave reviews.

Ethan and I also developed a Kaleido-Kit which is environmentally friendly, guaranteed, educationally powerful, and maintains the highest standards for optical quality and user safety.

Scott Cole

I have been developing the use of a variety of styles and materials in making kaleidoscopes since 1982. Specializing in custom scopes, I am a pioneer in the artistic use of blown glass and anodized aluminum bodies.

With a background in teaching, I enjoy sharing my enthusiasm and expertise by conducting kaleidoscope workshops. I am also a counselor by profession, and continue to explore the connections between creativity and personal growth.

Two scopes made with anodized aluminum encased in blown glass.

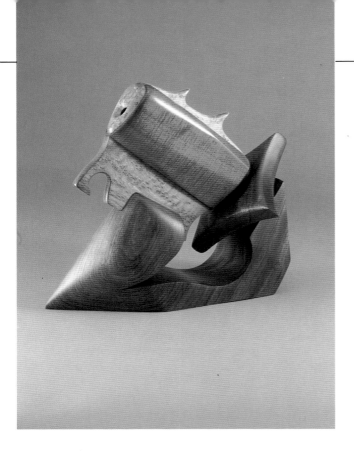

Carol Paretti

Kaleidoscopes are an exciting art form because they allow the artist to explore many different media while also investigating the technical aspects of the kaleidoscopic image.

Kaleidoscopes have magical, kinetic and sensory qualities to them. The exterior of the kaleidoscope can be something beautiful to look at, touch, and in the case of our aromatic cedar scopes, even smell. Then, while looking through a small aperature, you are able to enjoy a larger magical world of constantly changing color and form.

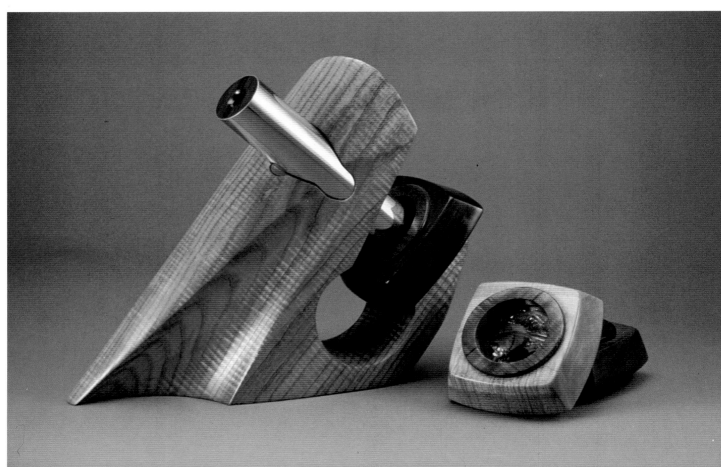

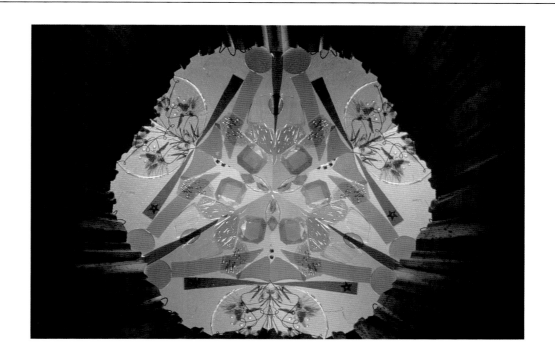

"Angler" (opposite top), "Whimsy" (opposite bottom), and "Series 640 Variation" (below), each made of exotic woods, with 2-mirror systems, fluted wood interiors and interchangeable object chambers. Photos by Terry Pemberton.

Alfred Brickel

Art is not held at arms' length. Art is inter-reactive—artist with medium—the discovery of a bright spirit within us, from child up.

The world's largest kaleidoscope. (Interior view, below)

Amy Hnatko

Because kaleidoscopes spend most of the time on tables or shelves, I wanted to create pieces that would be as beautiful to look at as to look through. When I began to make kaleidoscopes, there were few articles or books on the subject, so I had to solve the technical problems as well as the aesthetic ones. This led to many mistakes, but also to solutions which were uniquely my own. I tend to think three-dimensionally, and my designs often seem to spring into my mind in surprisingly complete detail. My many years spent working in stained glass gives me the experience to solve the structural problems. At some point during the construction, I have to let go of the initial idea and allow the piece to find its own form. My reward comes when my new design is finally completed—if it comes close to satisfying my original idea.

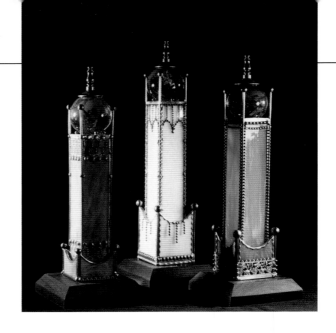

"Chinese Dragon" (below). Photo by Henry Tenbroeke.

"Xanadu Series" (above), with hand blown globes by Donna Fein. Photo by Amy Hnatko.

"Northern Lights" (opposite), with hand blown globe by Donna Fein. Photo by Henry Tenbroeke.

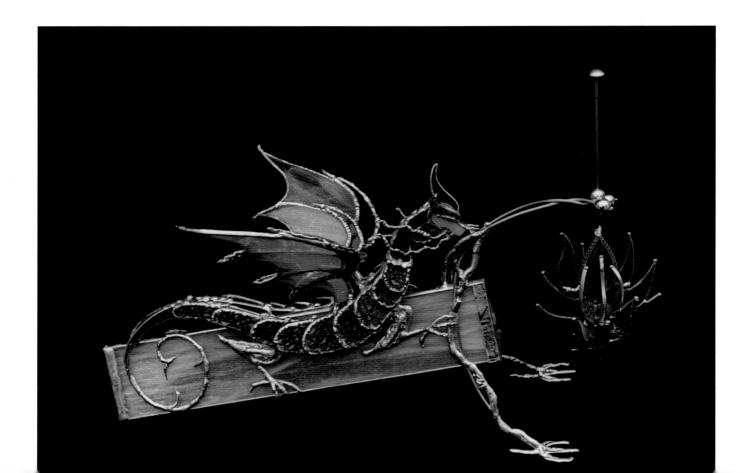

Sam Douglas

Kaleidoscopes offer me a synthesis of a lifetime's interests, experiences, techniques and abilities. This unique blend of instrument, toy and potential artwork—and the necessity for a kaleidoscope to fulfill a variety of roles—is challenging both technically and artistically.

No kaleidoscope is ever the same; no image repeats itself. Each work is both micro- and macro-cosm; it establishes its own ecology. That's why I call them Kaleidescapes, which combines the notion of "escape" with the ever-changing geography of a new landscape—an infinite journey in an eight-inch mirror. A twist of the wrist can alter the image utterly. The viewer of the scope becomes a collaborator, an image-maker as well.

My signature Kaleidescapes—the Empire State or Chrysler Building—contain a strange magic. It's a special moment to present such a piece and hear an adult laugh with a child's spontaneous delight at the mere sight of it…laugh at the idea of a secret world waiting inside a familiar form.

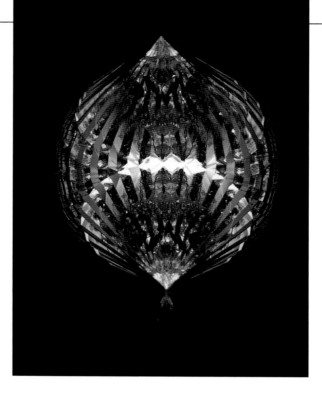

"Solar Wind" and "Crystal Phoenix" acrylic scopes (below), with interior images produced by Solar Wind (above) and Magna Sphere (opposite). Photos by Lawrence Tagrin.

Randy & Shelley Knapp

We believe we do more than produce kaleidoscopes; we give them life. By combining our talents in design, woodworking and sculpting, we create scopes that burst on the consciousness with color and light.

After settling our debts and quitting our jobs, we've devoted our energies to developing this art form. Our backgrounds in cabinetmaking, glazing, glass blowing, and even quiltmaking, have enabled us to produce unique scopes of the highest quality. We are always looking for new ways to utilize our technical skills and to put our heart and soul into each new design, which hopefully will endure through many generations.

"Verticulation" (above) contains 60 pieces of hand blown glass suspended in fluid to rotate vertically.

Interior image from "Twilight" (above).

"Twilight" (opposite top) features a unique side light object chamber containing flame sculpted dichroic glass and "stringerinis."

"Fly By" (opposite bottom) pivots in any position and can be detached from the base. Among the objects in its chamber are liquid filled ampules by the Falconers.

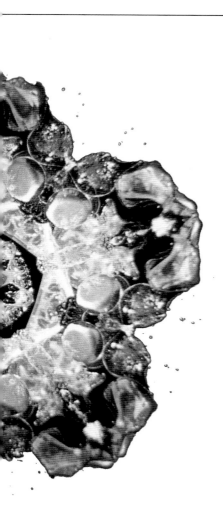

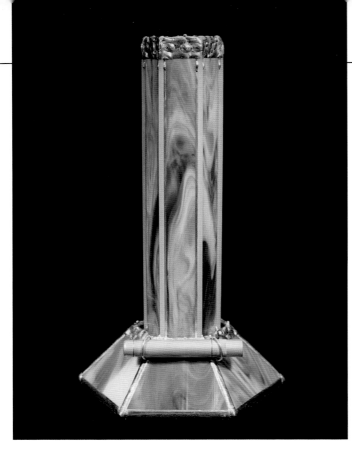

Sherry Moser

As a child growing up with a father who was a watercolor artist, color always held great fascination for me. I remember sitting beside him as he painted. It seems only natural that this color interest included the sparkling, changing images of toy kaleidoscopes.

As an adult, stained glass work is a stress-relieving hobby for my nursing profession. Stained glass rekindled my interest in color. Several years ago, I also discovered the wonderful world of contemporary kaleidoscopes. I put my glass skills to work and began creating my own kaleidoscopes.

The mandala images created by my pieces have special meaning for me. Mandalas have been used throughout history to promote balance, unity and healing, while also depicting the cyclic nature of life.

"Light Dancer" (opposite, top) on its base, with pen light viewing accessory.

Interior view of "Chandala" scope (opposite, bottom), with its 3-D dichroic effect.

"The Journey," with exterior and interior views. Photos by David Moser.

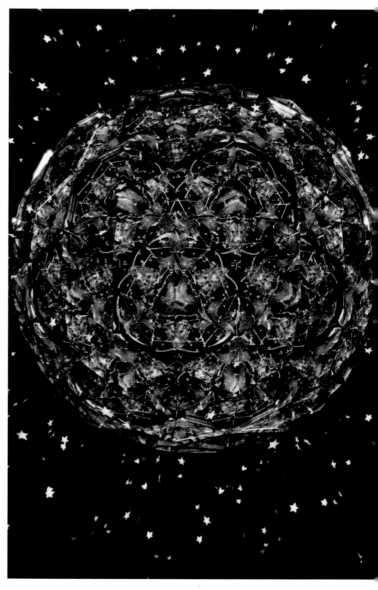

Dennis & Diane Falconer

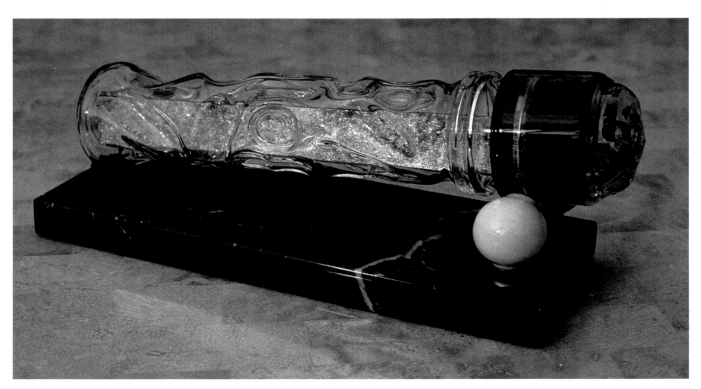

Styles of liquid filled ampules (above); colors are also varied.

"Ice Cave" (below) is made of handblown Pyrex glass and contains liquid filled ampules in a rotating, oil filled object chamber.

Our interest in kaleidoscopes developed over the years that we were collecting them. That interest turned to a love of the art form when I decided to make Diane an all handblown glass kaleidoscope, with liquid filled ampules, for our collection. It took my 25 years of experience as a scientific glassblower to accomplish this task. "Ice Cave" was truly a labor of love.

Since the limited edition "Ice Cave" we have developed other collector scopes. For these scopes, we chose to merge metal and wood together in our Fire Series. The fire refers to the polarized images. The colors correspond to the color of the exterior of each scope.

We spent a year developing and designing an array of multi-color filled ampules that are among the smallest ever created. As our scope designs unfold, these colorful components should enhance the value of our scopes.

Skeeter & Pete De Mattia

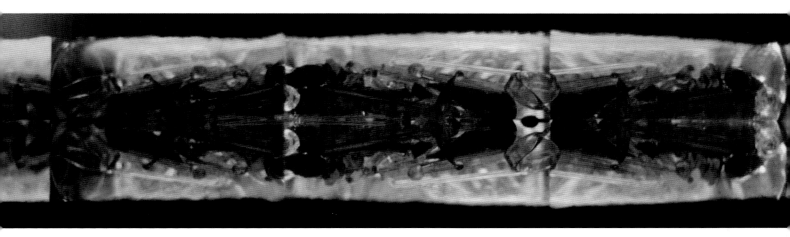

We are a husband and wife team, working out of the basement of our home. Five years ago we began collecting kaleidoscopes. Pete has had several vocations. He left his last job to devote full time to kaleidoscope making. Most recently he has been excited by a newly developed camera small enough to capture the interior of almost any kaleidoscope.

Necklaces were first. A glass tube acts as the reflective surface of the single dichroic wheel. Swirls of brilliant blues, pinks, and golds whirl before your eyes. Discovering irridized glass, we added a second wheel, which adds purples and greens to the images and alters the hues of the existing colors for a wondrous array of color. Color manipulation is the key to this scope. By rotating the wheels slowly, you can paint a palette of spiraling color.

From our excitement emerged the Warp Factor Series. Each scope in this series has a truncated, triangular shaped body. Warp Factor One is the first one-mirror scope known in existence. In Warp Factor Five, a unique vastness of space and light prevails, where columns arise, and "roads of light and color" come at you and recede into the distance.

Our most current design is the Warp Factor Two plus One, having a large spherical image with partial reflections adjacent to it. Ranking among the newer artists, we have a lifetime of ideas waiting to be made.

"Warp Factor" Series scopes.
(Interior of Warp Factor Three, above.)
Photos by Tess Scherer.

THE PRINCIPLES OF DESIGN

While kaleidoscopes may vary greatly in appearance and quality, there are four primary elements in any design:

1. the eye piece
2. the body
3. the mirror system
4. the object chamber

Each of these elements has its own set of variables, involving design configurations, dimensions, choice of materials, and construction techniques. Each combination of design elements produces its own unique image, which, in turn, produces endless variations from the objects being viewed.

The Eye Piece

The eye piece opening usually conforms to the shape of the mirror system in some way. It may open to the full viewing area, shrink toward the center or to one side, be shaped by external style considerations, be binocular, or even multiple if more than one mirror system is housed in the body. When designing your own scope, view the image through your prototype to best determine the appropriate placement, size and shape of the opening.

The other eyepiece consideration is the lens. You may choose to leave your eyepiece open, but be careful that the scope is handled most carefully so that loosened objects from the chamber or tiny chips of glass from the mirrors do not fall into your eye as you tilt it up for viewing. You may elect to cut a glass eyepiece, but again watch for breakage. The best option is plastic. Depending on your focal length, you may need an optical lens for magnification—either for tiny scopes or for visual effect. If your focal length is less than about 7 inches, you should use a lens for the specific distance between the eyepiece and the object chamber.

The Body

The kaleidoscope body merely houses the optical system, yet it should be regarded as the major external element in terms of visual presentation. The options are endless: round or faceted cylinders, tapered cylinders, flared or curved, and composed of any conceivable materials and added ornamentation. Another design consideration to be integrated with the construction of the body is the possible need for a stand or mount. If your scope is not free-standing (or lying), you may want to construct a cradle holder of similar material. Some bodies may incorporate legs of some kind to support them. A typical parlor-scope would be affixed to a stand at an angle, which might be adjustable. More elaborate mounts could involve belt-cranks or worm and tooth gears to either rotate the objects in the chamber or the angles of an adjustable mirror system.

The usual materials and construction techniques for creating kaleidoscope bodies are shown in the projects in this book: cardboard, plastics, metal, wood, and stained glass. Other possibilities include ceramic, fabric, blown glass, or any other material that can be fashioned into a rigid structure. The ornamentation of these surfaces can involve: various painting techniques (spraying, paper wrapping, marbleizing, stenciling, spinning, drip and splatter), gluing, soldering, etching, staining, inlay, glazing, sewing, etc.

The Mirror System

Mirror systems entail choice of material, dimension, angles and configuration. They are the soul of the kaleidoscope. You can experiment with acetate, metals, foil and mylar, especially if you are creating a cylindrical, spiral, or convex mirror system. Otherwise, you ought to consider 2nd or 1st surface mirrors. For optical quality, 1st surface mirrors are worth the extra investment. The overall size of your system may also be a factor.

The more crucial component for image production is mirror configuration. Two- and three-mirror systems are the most popular. Both are configured as a triangular cylinder, housed in some sort of tube.

The two-mirror system is shaped like a "V," with a 3rd side across the top that is blackened. The angle of the "V" determines the pattern of replication, as follows:

90°	-	4 images,	2 point star
60 °	-	6 images,	3 point star
45°	-	8 images,	4 point star
36°	-	10 images,	5 point star
30°	-	12 images,	6 point star
25.7°	-	14 images,	7 point star
22.5°	-	16 images,	8 point star
20°	-	18 images,	9 point star
18°	-	20 images,	10 point star
16.8°	-	22 images,	11 point star
15°	-	24 images,	12 point star

Three-mirror systems can be arranged in any form of triangle, and produce a continuous field of honeycomb-like patterns, so long as the sum of the three angles equals 180°. Here are three common patterns:

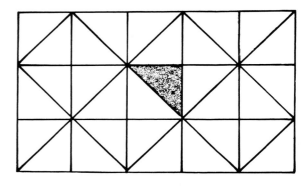

45° - 45° - 90°

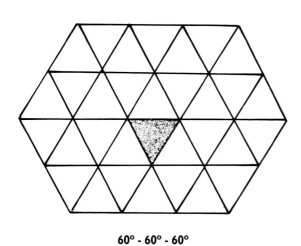

60° - 60° - 60°

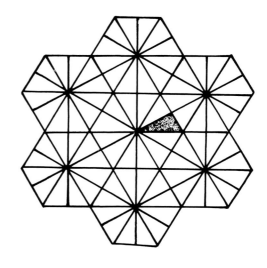

30° - 60° - 90°

Square, rectangular, and larger multiples produce images reflective of each shape. Tapered mirrors of three or more sides produce an interesting spherical image:

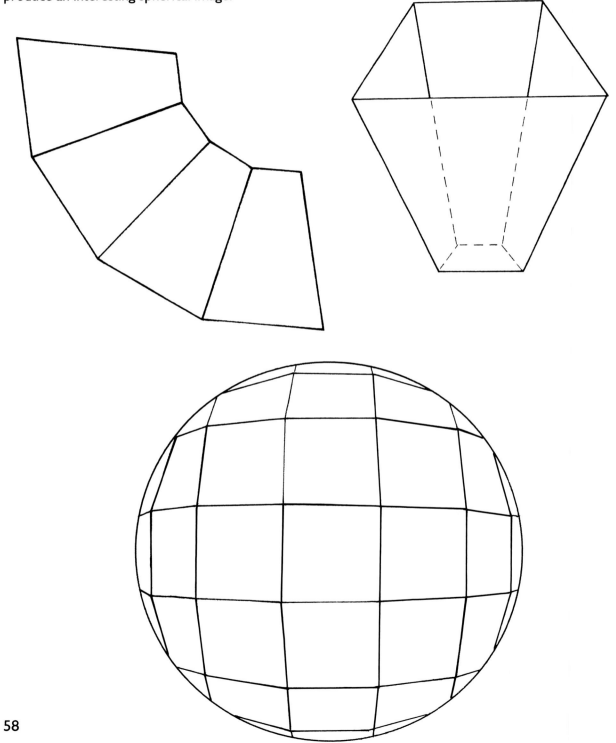

Cylindrical and spiral reflective surfaces will create images that reach through the barrel asymmetrically. Another option is to incorporate an apparatus for adjusting the angle of the mirrors (usually two) to achieve a range of image capability. It is also possible to contain two separate mirror systems within the body of the scope, each with its own eyepiece and viewpoint of the object chamber. Binocular systems have also been developed.

Mirrors can be mounted inside the body using any number of materials: foamcore, styrofoam, wooden strips, thick cloth; or they may be fit so exactly that a few spots of glue will suffice. The most common and effective way to join the mirror system is with duct tape.

The Object Chamber

If your scope is to be a teleidoscope, there will not be an object chamber, unless optionally attached for kaleidoscopic viewing. However, a teleidoscope can utilize lenses tht filter the light, such as with tinted, textured or faceted glass. Some chambers may be designed to be opened, for changing the objects inside. Others may be fixed to the body, so that the objects tumble as the whole body is turned. Still others have object chambers that rotate independently of the body, either in line or on a perpendicular axis. They may be detachable, interchangeable, containing colored fluids, or various add-on features.

The objects within the chamber are open to the imagination, yet are often coordinated with the exterior presentation of the scope in terms of color and texture. They may be composed of recognizable subject matter, abstract objects, or other fluid forms. They may be chosen for their color, shape, texture, weight, transparency, translucency, or opacity. There are alternative

formats, such as frames for 35 mm slides, drum and strip panoramas, and hand-drawn images as viewing objects.

With lighting properties and size as criteria, here are some possible objects for chambers:

broken colored glass and plastic

melted glass and plastic

broken auto windshields

mirror fragments

translucent stones and crystals

small polished stones

small colored beads

faceted and colored beads

tiny colored rods

small trinkets

small opaque objects

paperclips and metal fragments

various seashells

laminated flower petals, insect wings

marbles and ball bearings

sequins, glitter and stars

cellophane scraps

acetates: colored, frosted, scored

Having designed and composed the object chamber, there is the consideration of lighting. Mostly, your source will be natural light, but you may want the option of an artificial light source incorporated into your design—either fixed or moveable. Generally, light can be directed from the front and/or the side of the object chamber. It may also be diffused through a translucent pane, focused or bent through a lens, or filtered through tinted, textured, polarized, or dichroic glass.

BASIC CONSTRUCTION TECHNIQUES

Cutting Glass

This technique may seem a bit formidable to the novice, but can be mastered fairly easily with a little practice. You will need a glass cutter, a black felt-tip pen, a straight edge ruler, and some glass scraps to practice a few cuts.

First, measure and draw the exact shape onto the glass with the pen and the ruler, with lines extending fully to all edges. Place the glass on a table in front of you. Hold the glass cutter with the fingertips of both hands, lay the wheel on the far end of one of your longer marks, and draw it straight toward you down the mark until it rolls off the near edge (see Photo 1). The motion should be smooth and continuous with moderate, even pressure. You must score the glass only once for each cut. Keeping the wheel of your cutter oiled will prolong its life.

Once the glass is scored, grasp the near edge with thumbs over fists either side of the scored line, yet close together (see Photo 2). Rotate fists

firmly, with thumbs turning out from each other, pushing up from underneath to snap the glass apart and down the cut in one motion. Do not coax this process by first tapping under the scored cut with the ball end of the cutter, as other glass cutters do. This creates uneven edges unsuitable for mirror seams or stained glass joints. When cutting stained or textured glass, always score the smooth side. Also, be sure to wear safety goggles when cutting glass.

Cutting gentle curves utilizes this same technique. Severe and multiple curves are more difficult. To cut a disc, score and break a series of lines (as shown in the drawing), then even up the edge by chipping off irregularities with the notches in your glass cutter (see Photo 3).

Photo 2

Photo 1

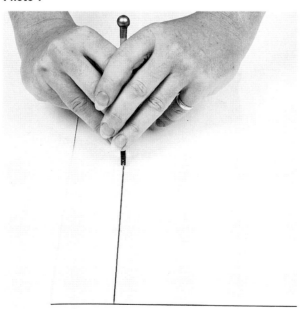

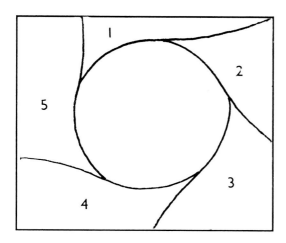

Since this is somewhat difficult, it is preferable to cut a disc from plexiglas using a fine tooth coping saw. Leave the adhesive backing on both sides until the cut is made. Edges can be smoothed, if necessary, with a file.

Photo 3

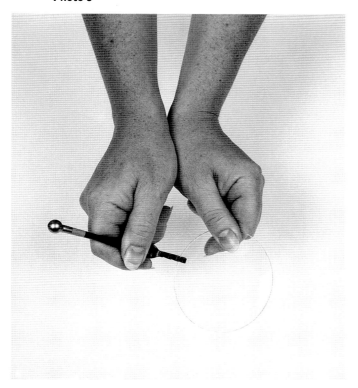

Joining Stained Glass

Your local stained glass or hobby shop can supply you with tools and materials for this operation. Having cut all your glass pieces, you should clean them with window cleaner or grease-cutting dishwashing liquid. Do be careful of sharp edges. Once thoroughly dried, wrap all the edges with copper foil (see Photo 4). Peel away a length of the adhesive backing, center the foil on an edge, press it and continue working your way around the perimeter, finishing with an overlap of about 1/4 inch. Then crimp the edges around both surfaces, making sure the foil adheres securely.

Practice the soldering technique on some scrap, to get the feel of it. First, using a flux

Photo 4

brush, apply "paste flux" to all surfaces of the copper foil. Then, place the tip of your soldering iron to the foil and touch the tip of some 50-50 solid core wire solder next to it until it flows over the foil (see Photo 5). Continue applying a thin coat of solder over the foil in a continuous motion around the edges until they are covered.

When all your pieces have been coated in

Photo 5

Photo 6

this way, you can assemble all or part of your structure using masking tape. Then, at the corners or other critical junctures, tack solder those spots by placing the tip of your iron on both edges to be joined, and touch your wire solder to the seam (see Photo 6). Allow just enough solder to flow into the joint to hold it together.

After soldering all these spots, your structure should be rigid enough to hold its shape. Gently remove the masking tape. Now you can continue soldering the rest of the seams, working your way around the structure in a step-wise motion, a half-inch or so at a time. Hold the iron and solder in place just long enough to fill the seam and form a smooth, rounded bead. If you stay too long, the solder may drip through the other side. Placing a wet paper towel on the other side up into the seam may prevent leaking solder and will assist your clean up. When all your seams are finished, wash off the flux with grease-cutting dishwashing liquid.

If you are soldering with mirrors in place,

such as attaching an eyepiece, you'll want to avoid getting flux inside your mirror system. First, clean all your surfaces, flux and coat the copper foil with solder, and clean again. Then dry tack your solder to create a continuous seam to seal the mirror system. Flux can then be applied to the exterior of these seams so that you can go back over them with solder to achieve a more attractive, finished seam.

Be careful to work in a well-ventilated area, handle the iron with care and unplug it when finished.

Working with Wood

Constructing a body or a stand out of wood can be as simple or as complex as you like. Even though one of the projects in this book requires a table saw to cut a rabbet, a simple flush cut edge would also suffice for a butt joint. Using a standard hand saw and a sand paper block, you can build a square cylinder kaleidoscope body by butting the edges together with glue.

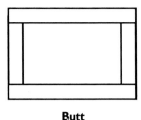

Butt

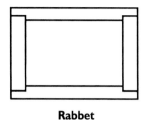

Rabbet

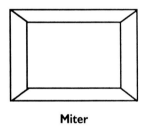

Miter

If you have a table saw, your cuts will be cleaner and more precise than with hand tools. Also, by adjusting the depth and angle of your cut, there are more options for joining the sides. You can also build cylinders that are triangular, hexagonal, tapered, or most any other shape. With more sophisticated tools and/or patience, the possibilities for ornamentation are also enhanced, such as carving, sculpting and inlay.

Your choice of woods is equally open. Thickness, stability, appearance and cost are all factors to be considered. Plywoods are available in many thicknesses and grades, some with attractive veneers. Pine is very accessible and can be stained many ways. Hardwoods are more expensive, but can be ordered from specialty lumber shops that can often plane it to your thickness specifications.

For best all around joining, use carpenter's wood glue. Clamps, weights, or even rubber bands can be used to achieve a tight seam. If you want to finish the wood with stain or clear finish, don't wipe the glue seams when wet. Rather, shave off excess glue with a knife and sand all over before finishing. There is a variety of stains, oils and finishes on the market, most of which will handsomely bring out the beauty of the grain and effectively protect it from years of handling.

It should go without saying that power-tools deserve respect. When working with small pieces of wood, keep your fingers away from moving blades by using push sticks or other aids. Bear in mind, too, that wood dust is good for neither your lungs nor your eyes. Wear an appropriate dust mask when working wood—and even consider wearing a respirator when sawing exotic species with powerful resins, such as walnut and cedar. Safety glasses should be a standard part of your attire.

Plastics and Metals

The plastic and metal projects in this book use standard, commercially available components. Generally, a diameter of tube or pipe is chosen that has commonly available fittings for the end pieces.

When cutting or drilling these materials, make sure you are using a blade or drill bit that is designed for that specific use. As always, power tools are more efficient and precise than hand tools, but both require caution and the usual safety practices.

There are many interesting materials worth exploring for your designs. Refer to the source guide in this book to get you started. Options for joining are varied, from gluing and welding to custom threading. Metals are usually polished and lacquered, but can be finished in many other ways, such as soldering, etching and enameling. Plastics can be altered for effect using coloration, texturing, and heat, among others. Experimenting with materials and techniques leads to new design possibilities.

Paper & Plastic Scope for Kids

Children have a natural appreciation for the "magic" of the kaleidoscope. There are many children who might apprentice themselves to a sorcerer just to learn how to craft this fascinating toy. Although this design uses only safe and simple materials for young hands, the skills and scientific principles acquired in the process are more than mere child's play. And the possibilities for design variation would challenge a wizard's imagination!

Materials List

Potato chip container - 9-3/4" tall, 3-1/8" diameter

2 plastic end caps (the 2nd from another chip container)

3" x 3" piece of 0.03" thick butyrate plastic

8" x 10" piece of 0.015" thick butyrate plastic

6" x 8-15/16" piece of white mat board

1/2" x 8-1/2" strip of corrugated cardboard

Packing material (styrofoam sheet or thick fabric)

Objects for viewing (plastic beads & fragments, trinkets, paper clips, etc.)

Spray adhesive

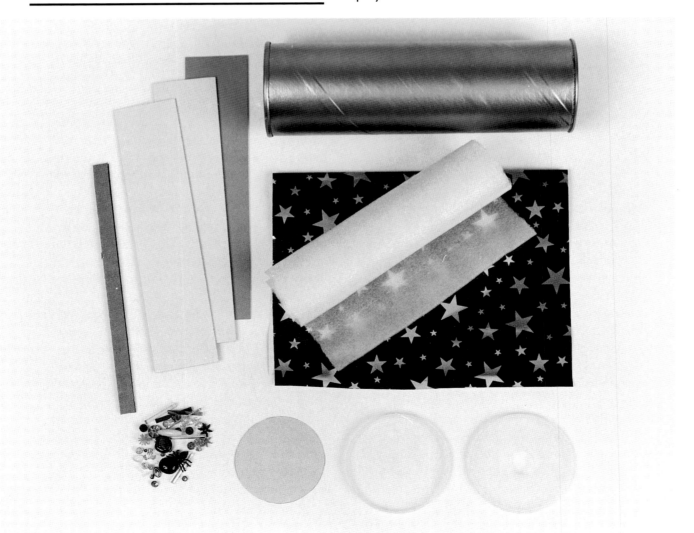

Here's how your scope might look on the inside.

Photo 1

Photo 3

1.   To prepare the potato chip container, remove (and eat?) the chips. Cut out the bottom with a can opener. This end will be used for the eye piece cap. Wipe out the inside of the tube so that it is as clean as possible.

2.   Decorate the tube. Use your imagination. You could spray paint it, cover it with paper and draw on it, wind ribbons or twine around it, cover it with cloth, or wrap it with gift wrapping paper (as shown in Photo 1).

3.   Make the eyepiece using one of the plastic end caps. Cut a hole, traced from a dime, in the center with small scissors or a utility knife (as

shown in Photo 2). Then cut a 2" x 2" piece of the thinner plastic (0.015" butyrate) and tape it to the inside of the cap to cover the hole. This will prevent any possible loose objects from the other end from falling in your eye. Now, snap it onto one end of the tube. (You may want to glue it in place.)

4.   To create the mirrors, first spray the white side of the mat board with an even coat of adhesive—not too much. Then press the thin (0.015) plastic onto it. Mark three adjacent rectangles, lightly with a pencil, on the plastic, each measuring 2" x 8-15/16". Cut these three strips as

Photo 2

Photo 4

66

Photo 5

neatly as you can with scissors or a utility knife.

5. To assemble the mirror system, lay the three mirrors, shiny side down, next to each other with 1/16" gaps between each long edge. Then tape across them with three 8" parallel strips of masking tape, so that you can fold the mirrors together and tape the last seam (as shown in Photo 3).

6. Wrap the assembled mirror system with packing material until it fits snugly into the tube. (See Photo 4.) Push it in until it fits flush with the eye piece.

7. To create the object chamber, cut a 2-

Photo 6

Photo 7

3/4" diameter circle from the 0.03" plastic with scissors. Then place it on top of the mirror system (as shown in Photo 5). Form the corrugated cardboard strip into a circle and place it on top of the plastic disc (as shown in Photo 6).

8. Pour some objects into this chamber (see Photo 7), but leave about 1/3 of the space empty so they can move around. Then snap the other end cap over the end to seal the object chamber. This cap can be removed to change the objects, or even left open to view the world through a teleidoscope. But for the kaleidoscopic effect, rotate the tube and watch the patterns change as the objects tumble.

Variations

Just like any other design in this book, all the major elements can be varied to create exciting new combinations and effects.

There are many sorts of cardboard tubes available: wrapping paper tubes, carpet and industrial ream tubes, even cardboard salt containers. End pieces can be fabricated from cardboard, and have different sized and shaped eye holes. The mirror angles can be variously configured. And, of course, there are always new objects to consider for the chamber: string, wood chips, pasta, ball point pen springs, rubber bands, styrofoam balls...virtually any small object that has interesting color, shape, texture and lighting qualities.

WHIRLING BUBBLE SCOPE FOR ALL AGES

*T**his wacky scope appeals to the child in all of us. It is composed primarily of found objects, and is quick and easy to make. Children can assemble it safely by substituting the plastic/cardboard reflectors used in the first project. The amazing special effect created by the pinwheel whirling behind the foaming bubbles is well worth an hour's effort.***

Interior view.

Materials List

Large plastic tumbler
Pinwheel
3 2nd surface mirrors: 1-3/4" x 4-3/8" (or to fit)
Plexiglass or 0.03" butyrate sheet: 3-1/2" x 6-1/2"
Bubble pipe
2 straws: straight and coiled
12" of 12 gauge copper wire (or heavy coathanger)

1. Drill an eye hole in the bottom of the tumbler about 1/2" in diameter. Cut a circle of plexiglass (with coping saw) or butyrate (with scissors) to fit inside the bottom of the tumbler (about 2-3/4" diameter), and glue it in place with plastic cement.

Photo
1

2. Find a recessed edge or any place near the lip of the tumbler, and cut another plastic circle to fit (about 3-1/2"). Measure the distance between these two plastic circles to determine the mirror length.

3. Cut 3 mirrors to this length and 1-3/4" wide, and assemble (see next project). Glue one end of mirrors, centered over eye hole, to the plastic circle in the bottom of the tumbler with silicone.

4. Place the larger plastic circle over the mirrors and glue the edge to the tumbler with plastic cement (see Photo 1).

5. Masking tape the bubble pipe to the tumbler, pointing in to center. Then tape the straight straw about 2" beside it.
Bend the wire into a "T":
Tape the top of the T
around the lip of the tumbler. Now secure all of this with duct tape (see Photo 2).

6. Cutting the ends to fit, insert the coiled straw into the bubble pipe, and tape the other end to the straight straw.

7. Bend tip of wire 90° and insert into stem of pinwheel, which has been cut to length so that the pinwheel will be visible through the mirrors. You can wrap the wire tip with duct tape to insure a snug fit.

8. The straight straw blows the pinwheel.

Drip bubble soap with a medicine dropper into the bubble pipe to blow bubbles into the viewing area.

Variations

The mirror configuration can be altered, even tapered. Pinwheels can be interchanged and embellished with different colors, sparklies, etc. Tape two together for a binocular effect. Look for other found objects.

Photo
2

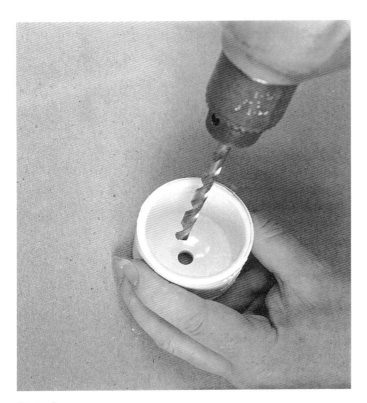

Photo 1

Photo 2

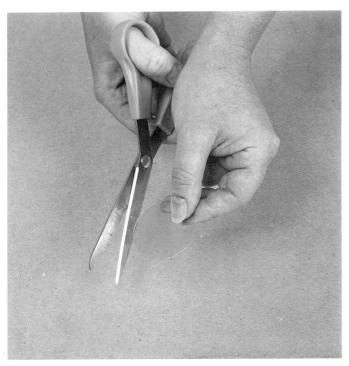

PLASTIC PIPE SCOPE FOR THE NOVICE

From computer micro chips to powdered orange drink, we've all seen how technologies developed for one use have found applications in many others. The scientists that invented PVC pipe may have imagined quite a few applications beyond plumbing, but kaleidoscopes? With ready-made fittings and tubing you can easily cut to any length, this design makes into a dandy scope that is durable, adaptable and professional-looking. And by substituting 1st surface mirrors with different angles and interchanging the objects in the open chamber, the quality and sophistication of your images is limited only by your imagination.

1. If you are cutting your own length of PVC pipe, you'll need to use a fine tooth blade, such as a hack saw or coping saw. Smooth the edges of the cut with a file and fine sand paper. Any ink lettering on the pipe can be rubbed off with steel wool.

2. In the center of the end cap, drill a 1/8" diameter hole to start the eye hole. Then change to a 5/16" bit and widen the hole (as shown in Photo 1).

Materials List

PVC pipe: 1-1/2" diameter, 9" long

PVC end cap: 1-1/2" diameter

PVC female adapter with threaded end: 1-1/2" diameter

1 sheet 0.03" Butyrate plastic: 2" x 4-1/2"

3 mirrors (2nd surface), each 1-1/8" x 10"

Styrofoam chips

3. From the sheet of butyrate, cut two circles, each 1-13/16" in diameter, and a third circle 1/2" in diameter (see Photo 2). Remove backing, if any.

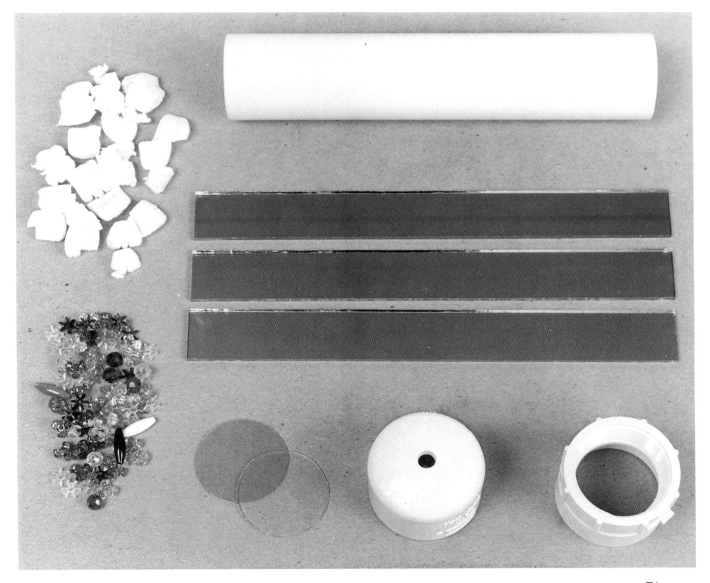

4. Using plastic cement, glue the small circle inside the end cap to shield the eye hole. Glue one of the larger circles inside the rim at the threaded end of the female adapter (as shown in Photo 3). Allow them to dry.

Photo 3

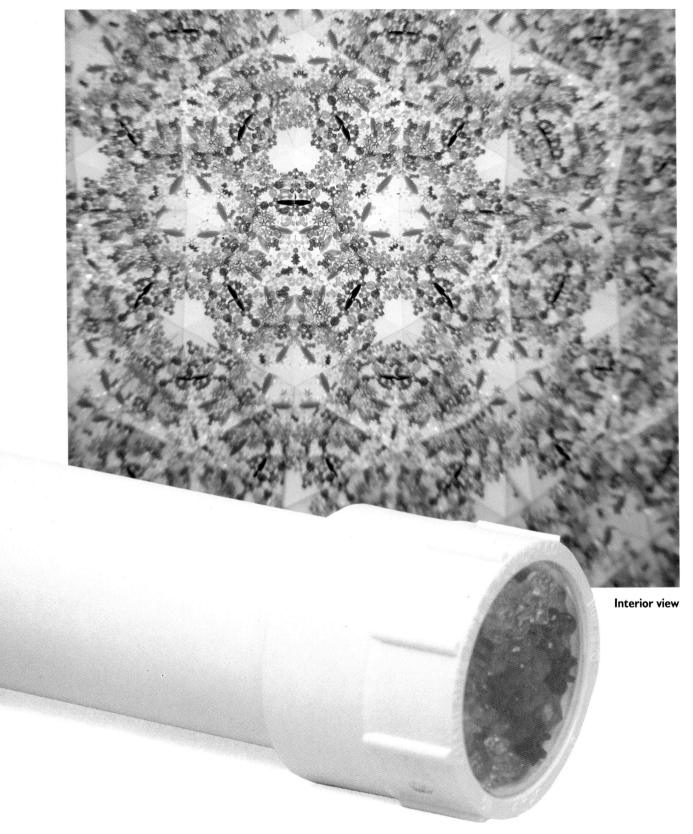

Interior view

Figure 1

Figure 2

5. Cut and clean the three mirror strips with window cleaner. Lay one of them on two strips of masking tape (see Figure 1). Position a second mirror (as shown in Figure 2), apply the tape and fold the mirror into a 60°. Position the third mirror so that the edges are aligned as in Figure 3, then wrap the tape all the way around. Further seal the assembly with duct tape, covering all the seams.

6. Place the end cap onto one end of the pipe, but not too tightly yet. Insert the mirror system partly into the pipe, and begin stuffing styrofoam chips equally around the three sides as you gradually insert the mirrors further. When the mirrors are fully inserted and packed, they should not slip out when inverted (see Photo 4). Mirrors should now be flush with the open end of the tube. Adjust the end cap (eye piece) to achieve this, if necessary.

Photo 4

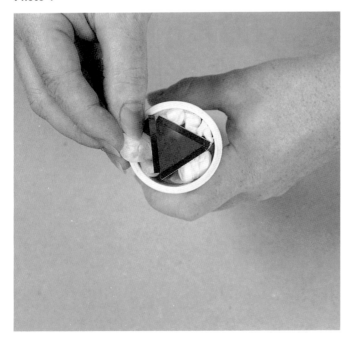

Photo 5

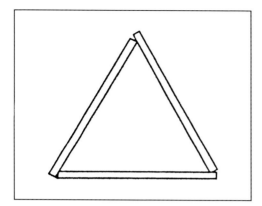

Figure 3

7. Place objects in the chamber (Photo 5) until they fill about 2/3 of the space up to the inner rim. Now place the remaining butyrate circle onto the inner rim (Photo 6), covering the objects.

8. The tube can now be inserted into the upper portion of the chamber, completing the scope. You may want to glue the eye piece permanently in place. The object chamber can be removed any time with a simple twisting motion, and opened to fill with new objects. It can also be removed to use your scope as a teleidoscope.

Variations

The eye hole can be larger. The pipe can be longer and/or larger diameter. It can be painted, carved, or accessorized with glue-on objects, wrapped with twine, etc. The mirror system can be varied many ways (see "Principles of Design"). The removable butyrate circle in the object chamber can be interchangeable with other sorts of tinted or textured pieces—even faceted discs or curved lenses. These can also be used without any objects in the chamber to alter the teleidoscopic effect.

Photo 6

Photo 7

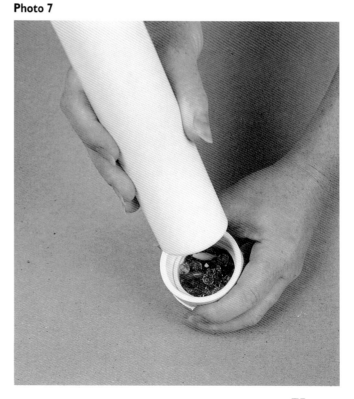

CLASSIC BRASS TELEIDOSCOPE

*Y*ou may notice the resemblance between this elegant scope and some of its antique predecessors. A major difference, however, is that this design has no object chamber. It is a teleidoscope. So whether you are viewing autumn foliage (below) or the beach at Waikiki (opposite), the world is your object chamber. Give this design a try, and you'll discover how such a simple approach can open so many exciting viewing possibilities.

Interior views through a 3-mirror system.

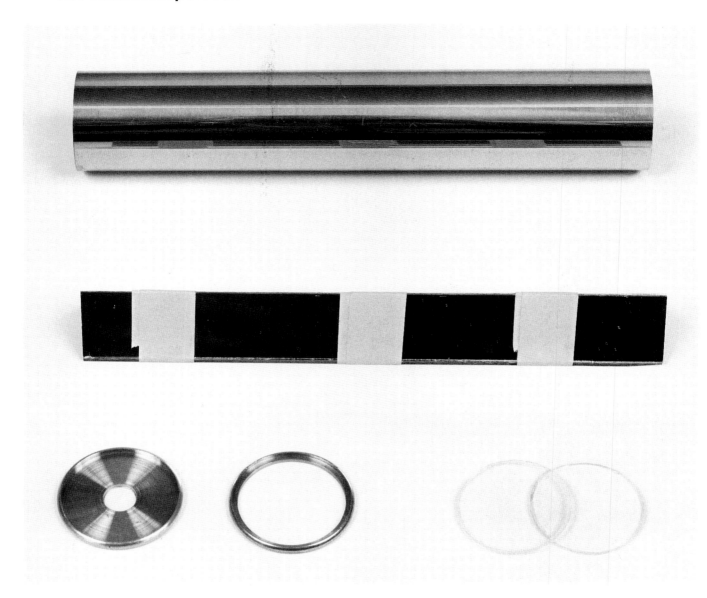

Materials List

Brass tube: 1-1/2" diameter, 8-1/4" long
3 1st surface mirrors: 1" x 8"
Plexiglass or glass sheet: approx. 2" x 4"
2 brass fittings
Packing material (styrofoam or thick cloth)

Note

If you have difficulty obtaining brass tube or fittings, consult the Source Guide in the back of this book. However, the measurements of all parts can be adjusted to suit whatever materials you can find.

1. If your brass tube has already been polished and lacquered, it is advisable to protect it during construction. Wrap it with newspaper, leaving 1/2" bare at each end, and secure with tape. If the brass is unfinished, you may also wrap it, take care in gluing, and buff and lacquer it after construction. Make sure all brass fittings are clean before gluing.

2. Cut the three mirrors, and assemble the mirror system as shown in the plastic pipe project.

3. Before you insert the mirror system into the tube, wrap it with packing material so that it will be centered and fit snugly. You can also stuff packing material, such as styrofoam strips or chips, around the mirrors as you insert them (as shown in Photo 1). One end of the mirrors should be almost flush with the tube, the other end recessed about 3/16".

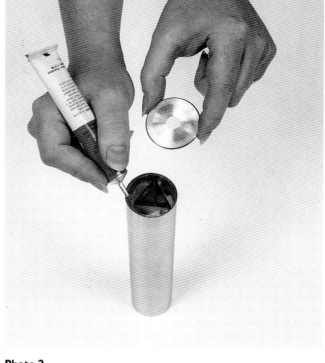

Photo 2

Photo 1

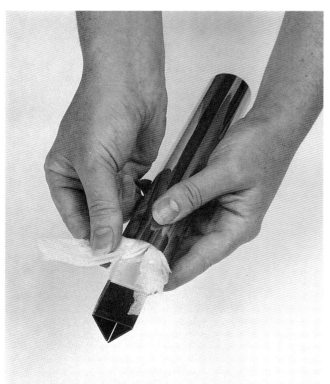

4. Cut two lenses, each 1-7/16" in diameter. Use a fine tooth coping saw to cut the plexiglass, or a glass cutter to cut glass, as described in "Construction Techniques." These should fit inside the brass tube. Clean the lenses.

5. Stand the tube up on the recessed end. Lay a lens on top of the mirrors so that it rests flush with the top of the tube. Using 5-minute epoxy and following the gluing directions on the container, glue the edge of the lens to the rim of the tube. (See Photo 2) Then glue the eye piece onto this end. Let dry.

6. Stand the tube up on the other end. If you want to conceal the packing material between the mirrors and the tube, you can stuff black paper over the top. Now lay the other lens on top of the recessed mirrors, and glue the edge to the inside of the tube to seal it (as shown in Photo 3). Avoid spilling glue onto the lens surface where it will be visible.

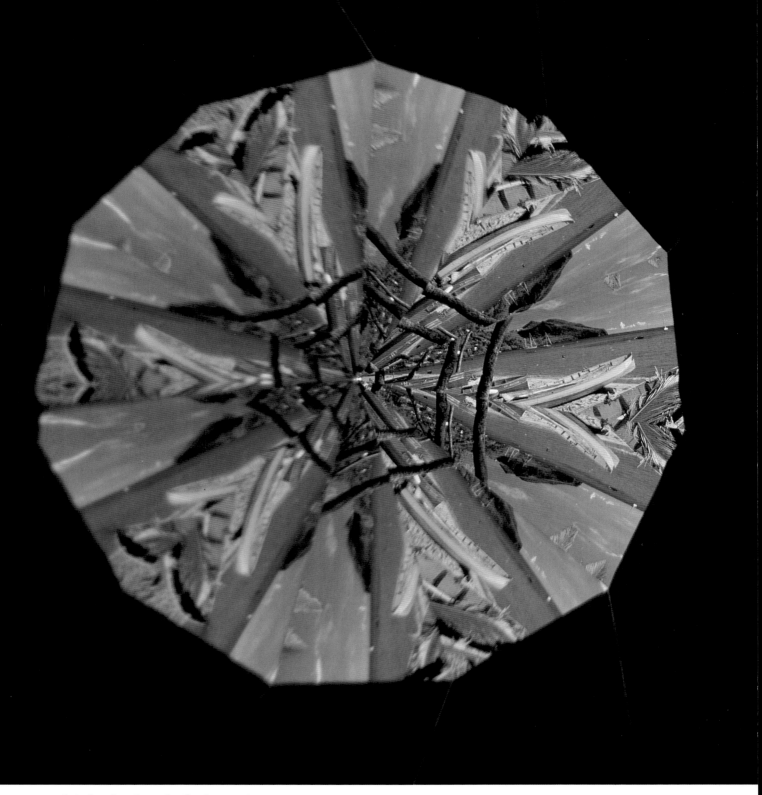

Interior view through a 2-mirror system.

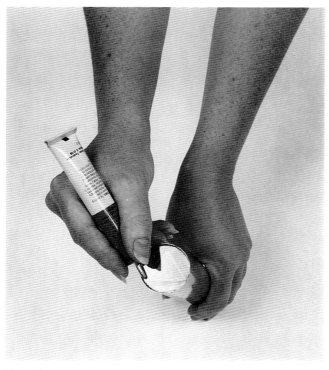

Photo 3

Photo 4

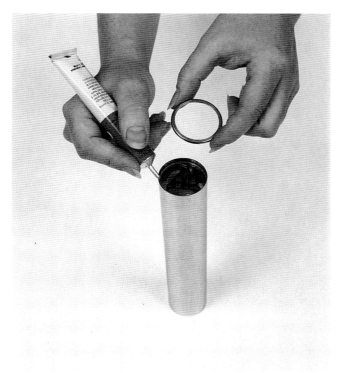

7. Glue the end cap onto this end (as shown in Photo 4). Let dry. Unwrap and/or finish the brass surfaces with polish and clear lacquer. Or try etching the brass decoratively.

8. You may want to cut out plastic discs of different tints and textures which can be slightly bent to fit into the recessed end of your scope. Leave a tab on one edge for easy removal. (See photo on page 76.)

Variations

Since the teleidoscope lacks the usual object chamber options, lenses become an important design element with which to experiment. In addition to colored, polarized and dichroic filters, various textures and facets on the surface of a lens can affect the image in many ways. Also, by attaching a curved lens—even a hemisphere—the potential for image distortion enters a new dimension.

If you were to thread the end of your tube for a screw-on end cap, you could make an assortment of interchangeable mirror systems. (see "Principles of Design.") The end lens would not be glued, but held in place by the end cap. Each mirror system would need to be measured carefully for a snug fit, without packing material. The photo (opposite) shows how a typical 2-mirror system might look.

Most of all, you can enjoy looking at usual sights in an unusual way. Moving objects are especially fascinating: water waves, smoke plumes, rustling leaves or flowers, billowing clouds, tongues of flame, flashing neon lights, etc. Imagine switching off between your opera glasses and a teleidoscope at the ballet, or viewing a fireworks display, or one of those Christmas baubles with the shake-up snow scene inside, or...

MINIATURE KALEIDOSCOPE PENDANT

The interior image
has surprising detail (opposite right).

Actual scope length: 2-3/4"

*T*he beauty of this tiny brass scope is its portability, but the quality of its image will amaze you. The more you grow to appreciate the joy of scope viewing, the more you'll wish you had one with you at various moments of the day. Whether you carry it on a necklace, a key chain, or fix it on a tie clip, the images are always within reach to soothe or stimulate. And as a teleidoscope, you can explore the many sights you encounter wherever you travel.

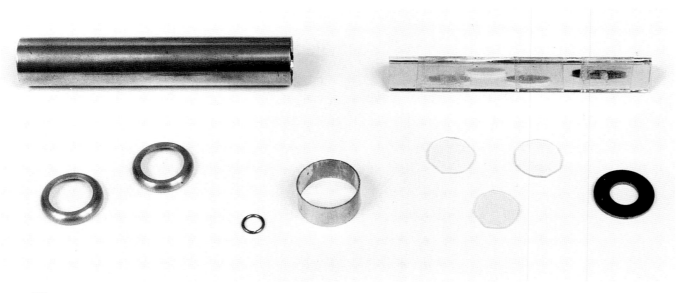

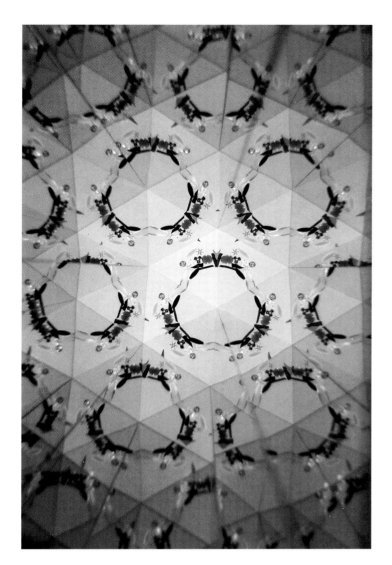

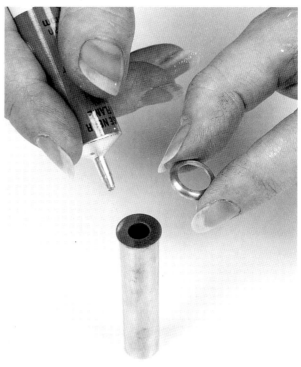

Photo 1

Photo 2

Materials List

Brass tube: 1/2" diameter, 2-3/4" long
3 1st surface mirrors: 3/8" x 2-3/8"
2 brass fittings: 1/2" (lamp base rings)
Small brass eyelet ring
Brass collar: 9/16" diameter, 1/2" long
Brass washer: 1/2"
0.03" butyrate or thick acetate sheet: 1" x 1"
Plano-convex lens: 10 mm x 90 mm FL

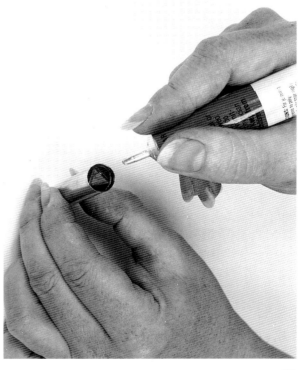

1. Follow the procedures concerning brass surfaces as described in the brass teleidoscope project.

2. Cut and assemble the three mirrors. You can align the seams more easily with household cellophane tape. Then wrap the mirror assembly with duct tape until it fits snugly inside the brass tube.

3. You can use the optical lens from a peep hole "door viewer," or order one from a supplier in the Source Guide. If it is plastic and larger than 15/32" diameter, you can file it down to size.

4. Apply a thin bead of 5-minute epoxy around the outer perimeter on the flat side of the lens. Then glue it, centered, on the washer. Let dry.

5. Apply a bead of epoxy on one of the rims of the brass tube. Carefully insert the lens and washer, curved surface facing inside, to glue it in place. Apply a bead of epoxy inside the lip of a brass fitting, and glue it over top (see Photo 1). Let dry.

6. Insert mirrors into tube. With scissors, cut two circles from the 1" square plastic sheet, each 15/32" in diameter. Place one of these on top of the mirrors inside the tube, and glue it in place (as shown in Photo 2). Avoid getting glue on the mirrors or in the viewing area of the plastic circle. Let dry.

7. The brass collar can be cut from tubing. Solder the small eyelet onto the collar (see Photo 3), although not in position around the tube as shown. After cleaning the ring and collar assembly, it should be placed around the tube (as shown).

8. Place small beads and fragments of broken stained glass into the object chamber (as shown in Photo 4). Fill about halfway full.

Photo 3

Photo 4

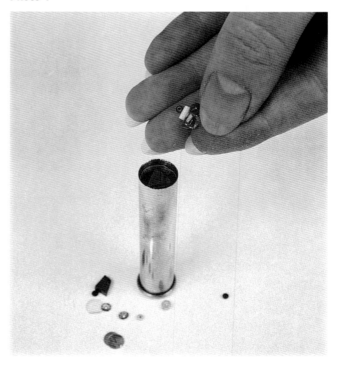

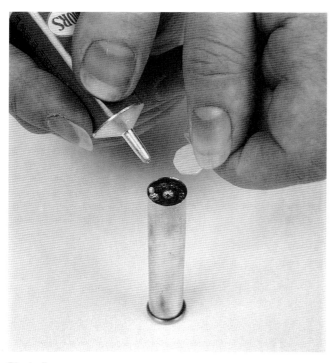

Photo 5

Photo 6

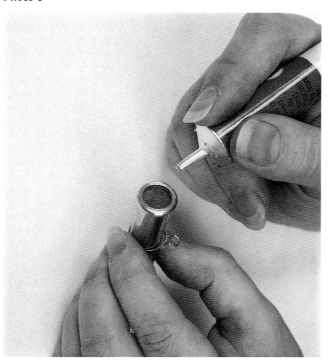

9. Frost the other plastic circle using fine sandpaper until it is uniformly cloudy and translucent.

10. Apply a bead of epoxy on the rim of the brass tube (see Photo 5), taking care not to glue any of the objects in the chamber. Gently place the frosted circle into the rim, so that it is perfectly flush with the top of the tube. Let dry.

11. Apply a bead of epoxy inside the lip of the other brass fitting, and glue it in place over the end of the object chamber (as shown in Photo 6). Let dry.

12. You may want to polish this brass scope every so often. A protective coat of clear lacquer is not advisable, since the collar around the tube will scratch it off unevenly, leaving marks to tarnish. Another option would be to solder the eyelet ring directly onto the tube.

Variations

To make a teleidoscope with this design, cut the mirrors 1/16" shorter than the brass tube. Use clear plastic lenses (not curved) on the ends, and follow the same basic procedures used in the brass teleidoscope project. There's no need to recess the object end for extra lenses, although permanently attaching a curved or hemispheric lens to the object end would produce interesting effects.

You also have the option of employing different sorts of mirror systems in either kaleidoscope or teleidoscope. The scope is probably too small to incorporate the option of interchangeable mirror systems, although you could carry several of these scopes with you—each with its own system. If a sheet of brass or copper were formed into a cone, a tapered mirror system could be accommodated.

WONDERFUL WOODEN SCOPE

As simple as making a box, this woodworking project shows you the basics so you can go on to all sorts of more ambitious design variations. You'll also be introduced to a unique mirror system: two tapered mirrors that produce a "chorus line" effect. Wood has such warmth and natural beauty, we were inspired to fill our object chamber with a mixture of earthy baubles amongst the glittery ones: stones, sea shells, mother-of-pearl, bamboo and crystals.

Materials List

2 pieces of wood: 1/4" x 1-3/4" x 9"

2 pieces of wood: 1/4" x 1-1/2" x 9"

2 pieces of wood: 1/4" x 5/16" x 1-1/4"

1 piece of wood: 1/4" x 1-3/4" x 1-3/4"

2 1st surface mirrors: 1-1/4" x 7-7/8"

1 piece of 1/16" window glass: 1" x 1"

1 piece of 1/16" window glass: 1-1/4" x 1-1/4"

1 piece of white plexiglass: 1-1/4" x 1-1/4"

2 pieces of white plexiglass: 1/2" x 1-1/4"

5" of 14 gauge brass wire

5" of double face glazing tape

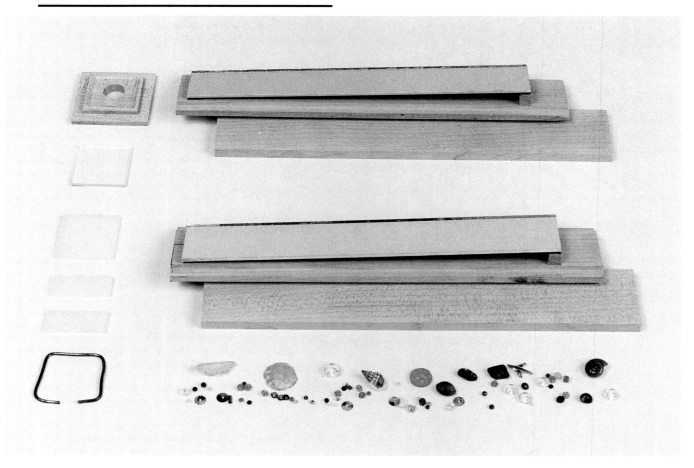

1. On a table saw, cut two pieces of 1/4" stock (most any wood you like) to 1-3/4" x 9". Set your saw to a 1/8" depth of cut, and rip cut a 1/4" rabbet down each long side. (See "Basic Construction Techniques" for other joinery options.) Now cut two more pieces of 1/4" stock

Photo 1

to 1-1/2" x 9". (Photo 1) You may want to paint one side of each of these two plain panels flat black for a more striking effect. Note all edges to be glued and mask these margins from the paint for a better glue joint. Lightly sand new edges.

2. Carefully, using a push stick, rip cut a length of 1/4" stock to a width of 5/16". Then cut two lengths, 1-1/4" each. These are the mirror blocks.

3. Mark one end of each of the two rabbet-cut pieces with two parallel lines: 7/8" and 1-1/4" in from the end. Glue the 1/4" surface of each mirror block inside these lines.

4. Cut two mirrors, 1-1/4" x 7-7/8" each. Install the mirrors carefully, with one end flush with the mirror block (as shown in Photo 2) using 1-1/4" strips of double face glazing tape.

5. Run a bead of glue into all four rabbet cuts, and distribute evenly with your finger. Set the two mirror panels on top of a plain panel (see Photo 3), then gently lay the other plain panel into the rabbet cuts on top. Secure the assembly with rubber bands (see Photo 4) and allow 4 hours to dry. If you plan to use a natural wood finish, don't wipe the excess glue at the seams. Instead, shave off excess with a knife after it has dried, then sand.

6. To cut the eye piece, cut a 1-3/4" x 1-

Photo 2

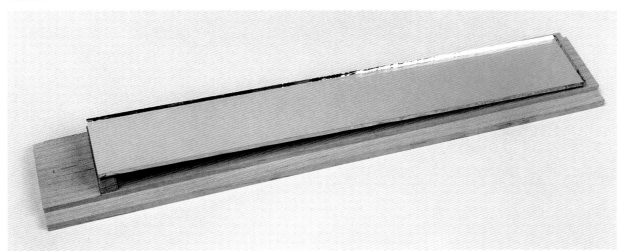

3/4" piece of 1/4" stock, then cut a 1/4" rabbet, 1/8" deep, all the way around. Drill a 1/2" hole in the center (see Photo 5), then sand all new edges.

7. Cut a 1" square of window glass, clean it, and glue it over the inside of the eye hole (see Photo 6) with silicone. After this has dried, you can glue this eye piece into the end of the tube without the mirror blocks using wood glue (see

Photo 7). Allow it to dry, then sand the whole body to your liking.

8. Cut a 1-1/4" square of window glass, clean it, and glue it against the mirror blocks (see Photo 8) with silicone. This forms the inside object chamber window.

9. Cut two pieces of 1/2" x 1-1/4" white plexiglass spacers using a fine tooth coping saw or hack saw. Glue these in place above the mir-

Photo 3

Photo 4

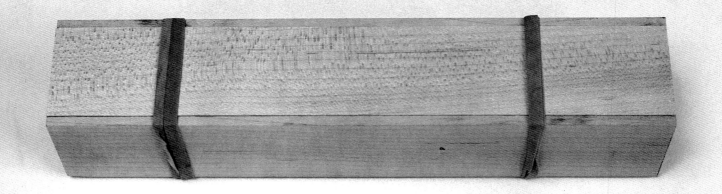

ror blocks (see Photo 9) with silicone.

10. Cut a 1-1/4" square of white plexiglass for the object chamber lid. This is dropped into place, but never glued (see Photo 10).

11. Bend a piece of 14 gauge brass wire around a 1-1/16" square block to make the lock spring (see Photo 11). Then force it into place

Photo 7

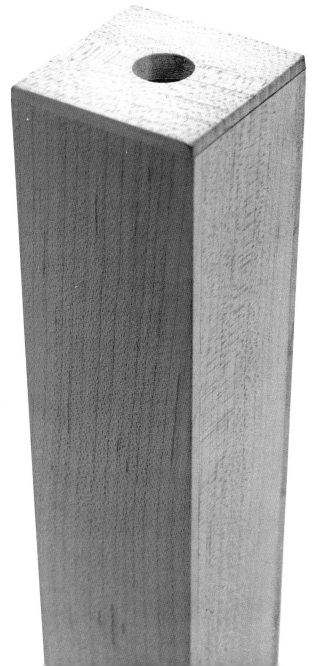

Photo 5

Photo 6

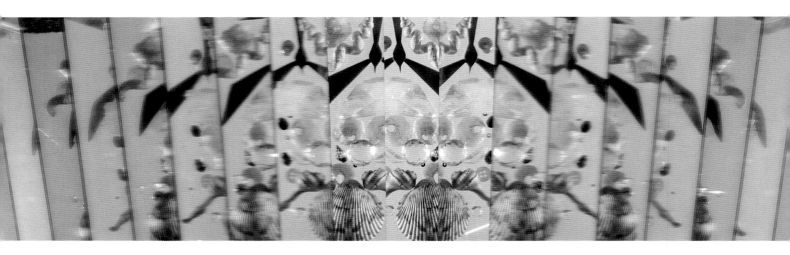

"Chorus line" effect inside the tapered two-mirror system (opposite).

Interior view of standard three-mirror system (below).

Photo 8

Photo 10

Photo 9

Photo 11

over the lid (as shown in Photo 12).

12. To insert and change objects, simply unspring the lid and replace it. The chamber may, of course, be left open for use as a teleidoscope. This would also include viewing 35 mm slides or film strips.

Variations

You may want to incorporate different woods in the body—perhaps add some carving or inlay, or try different stains. The corners can be rounded with a router as a more comfortable handheld feature. Obviously, wood allows you much freedom to experiment with different sizes and shapes.

Mirror systems can be varied any number of ways. For a standard three-mirror system, join three strips of mirror, 1-1/6" x 7-7/8" each. Attach a corrugated cardboard shim with two long strips of double face glazing tape (see Photo 13). When assembling the body, leave out the mirror blocks. Slide the mirrors into the body, and install both end piece assemblies as before. For tighter angled mirror systems, you may need to adjust the size and position of the eyehole.

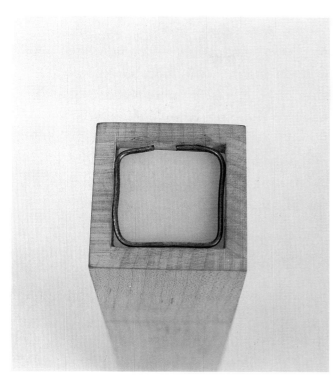

Photo 12

Photo 13

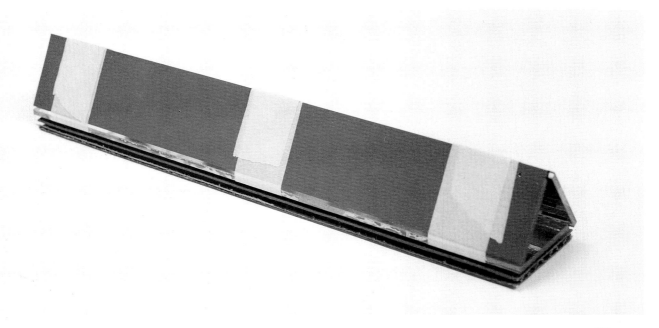

STAINED GLASS TWO-MIRROR SCOPE

*T*here is much beauty in the simplicity of this scope—inside and out. Except for the foil and solder, it is composed entirely of glass. The colors you choose for your scope can be attuned to the disposition and yearnings of your spirit, or to the friend for whom you make it. And the two-mirror system, preferred by many, produces the spectacular "mandala" image that is sure to hold you spellbound.

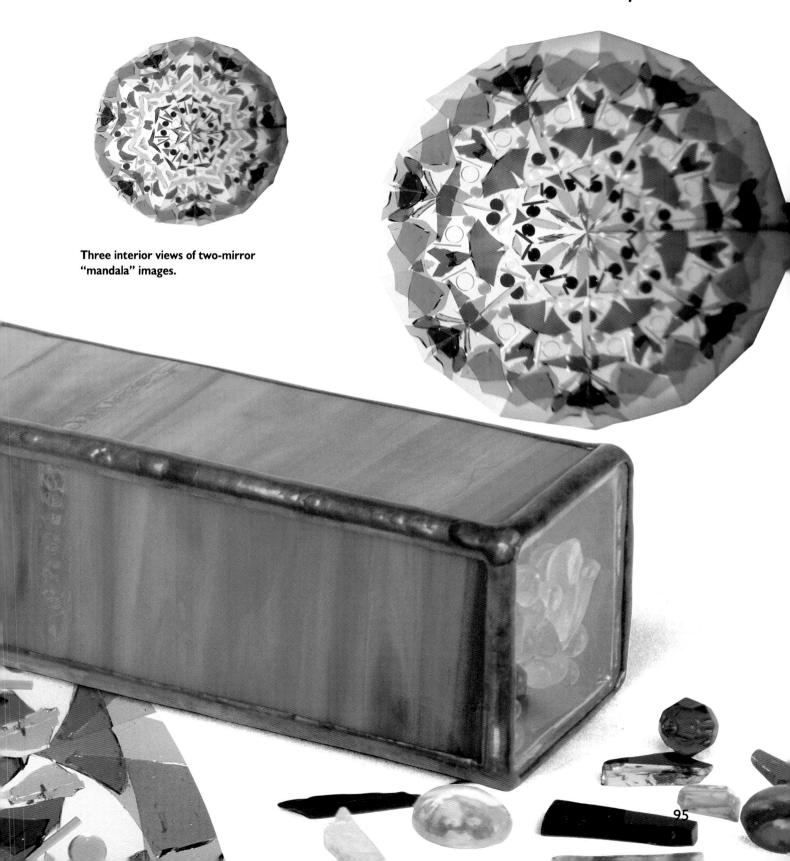

Three interior views of two-mirror "mandala" images.

95

Materials List

4 strips of stained glass: 1-1/4" x 8"

2 1st surface mirrors: 1-3/16" x 7-1/2"

1 mirror glass: 5/8" x 7-1/2"

1 piece of stained glass: approx. 1-1/2" square

1 piece of clear glass: approx. 1-1/2" square

1 piece of clear glass: approx. 1-1/4" square

1 small scrap of clear glass for eye piece

1 strip of black velvet or felt: 5/8" x 7-1/2"

1.   Cut four strips of stained glass, 1-1/4" x 8" each. (See "Basic Construction Techniques" for all stained glass assembly.) Clean the glass, and wrap all the edges with copper foil (see Photo 1). Brush on the paste flux, then coat all the foil with solder. Clean off the flux.

2.   Assemble the four panels into a cylinder and secure them with masking tape. Tack solder the four corners on each end (as shown in Photo 2). The structure should hold its shape as you gently remove the masking tape. Now you can flux and solder all the seams. Clean off flux, inside and out, when you're done.

3.   Cut two mirrors, 1-13/16" x 7-1/2" each. Cut another strip of mirror or glass 5/8" x 7-1/2". Cover this smaller strip with an equal strip of

Photo 1

black velvet or felt using spray adhesive (see Photo 3).

4. Lay the two larger mirrors, 1st surface side down, 1/8" apart. Gently apply duct tape down the seam (as shown in Photo 4). Cut a 7-1/2" length of duct tape about 2" wide, and lay it

Photo 2

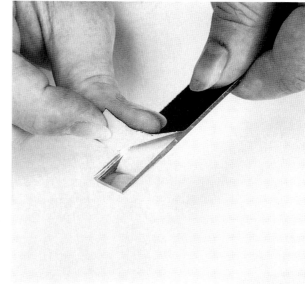

Photo 3

on a table, sticky side up. Lay the smaller panel, black surface up, in the center of the tape. Fold the larger mirrors into an acute angle, tape facing outside, and place them over the black panel to create tight seams with the black panel fitting flush inside the top of the "V." Wrap the tape

Photo 4

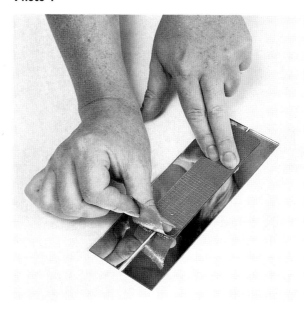

Photo 5

Photo 6

around both seams (as shown in Photo 5). The mirror assembly should fit snugly inside the square cylinder. Wrap more tape if necessary. The mirrors should be flush with one end of the cylinder, recessed on the other. (See Photo 6)

   5. Cut a piece of clear glass that will just fit

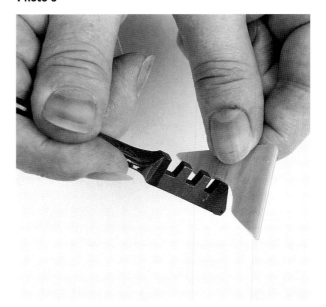

Photo 7

Photo 8

inside the recessed end of the cylinder, approximately 1-1/4" square. Mark the actual opening to allow for any inconsistencies, and leave space for the foil. Clean the glass square, wrap it with foil, coat the foil with solder, clean it again, and then tack solder it into the recessed end of the cylinder at all four corners (as shown in Photo 7).

6. Cut a piece of stained glass to fit the flush end of the cylinder. Then cut it diagonally into two pieces. Cut an arc inside the long edge of each piece, refining the edge by chipping at it with the teeth of your cutter (see Photo 8). Now cut a small football-shaped piece of clear glass that will fit inside these two arcs. Foil and join these three pieces into a square to serve as the eye piece.

7. Clean the eye piece, then dry tack it onto the flush end of the cylinder. Flux is not used until the end is sealed, so as not to foul the mirrors, but can be used afterwards to make a prettier seam (see Photo 9).

8. Cut a piece of clear glass to fit the recessed end of the cylinder. Prepare it for joining. Fill the object chamber about 1/2 to 2/3 full with small colored glass fragments and globules, or anything else you like. The object chamber

will remain closed, so choose carefully. Dry tack the clear square over the end using the same method as the eye piece. After cleaning away the exterior flux, the solder can be finished with copper sulphate if you wish.

Variations

This basic design lends itself to many variations: size and shape of the eye piece; size, shape and color of the body; most any sort of mirror configuration; perhaps a hinged lid covering the object chamber so that the objects may be changed; an object chamber that has side-lighting with an opaque end and clear sides; using filtered glass in the object chamber or in place of the black mirror panel; objects that tumble inside the entire length of the mirror system…explore the possibilities!

Photo 9

Photo 10

STAINED GLASS WITH WHEELS

Materials List

Body

3 panels of stained glass: 1-1/2" x 8"

2 clear glass triangles: 1-7/16" sides

3 1st surface mirrors: 1-1/4" x 7-7/8"

Brass rod: 1/8" diameter, 3" long

3/8" brass ball with threaded hole

2 brass eyelets (for legs)

Chamber

6 stained glass rectangles: 1/2" x 1-1/2"

2 clear glass hexagrams: 1-1/2" sides

Brass tube: !/8" diameter, 3/4" long

Disc

Several stained glass pieces to fill 3" circle

Brass eyelet

*S*tained glass lends itself beautifully to scope making. This design exploits the properties of color and light with glass wheels that function as external object chambers. Basic stained glass technique enables easy construction of the wheels in both two and three dimensions, and all are interchangeable. Select the colors of glass you like, practice your joinery skills, and give this scope a whirl.

Photo 1

The Body

1. Foil and join the stained glass panels into a triangular cylinder. (See "Construction Techniques.")

2. Thread one end of the brass rod to accommodate the brass ball. Solder the other end of the rod into one of the seams at the end of the stained glass cylinder. Leave 1-3/8" of the rod extending beyond the end of the cylinder.

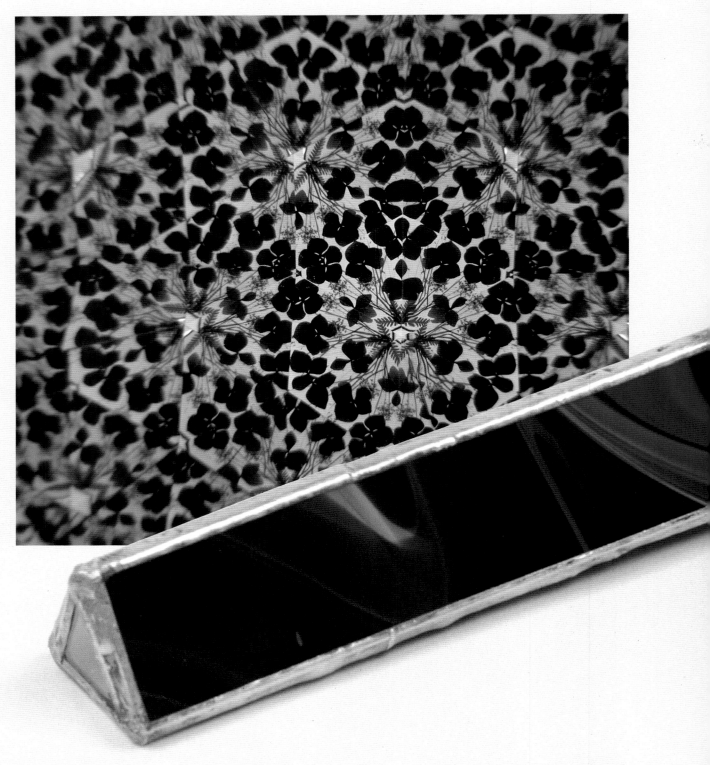

**Interior view of flower disc
through 3-mirror system (above).**

**Chamber wheel with stained glass contents
and two detachable discs..**

3. Now solder the two brass eyelets into the other two seams of the cylinder at the same end (see Photo 1). Flux and smooth out all solder seams, and clean.

4. Cut and assemble the mirrors.

5. Insert the mirror system into the cylinder, using packing material to center it with a snug fit (see Photo 2). Leave equal margins of recess at each end of the cylinder.

6. Foil both clear glass triangles, and solder them into each end of the cylinder to seal the mirror system (see Photo 3). Be careful to use dry solder techniques, so as not to foul the mirrors. Foil can be added to secure the seal. Refine the seams, and clean. This completes the body.

The Chamber

1. Foil and join the six stained glass rectangles into a hexagram (see Photo 4) by spot soldering the corners.

2. After you've cut the two clear glass hexagrams, frost one of them with fine sand paper to make it translucent.

3. Cut both of the hexagrams into sixths, creating six triangles from each (see Photo 5). Carefully chip or grind off one corner of each triangle to accommodate a 3/16" hole for the

Photo 2

Photo 3

brass tube in the center.

4. Foil all 12 triangles, and join back into two hexagrams, one clear and one frosted, each with center hole space.

5. Solder one of the hexagrams to the stained glass side assembly. Insert the brass tube upright into the hole, and solder in place. Solder the seams between the six stained glass sides. Clean the interior. (Note: Two eyelets could be used in place of the tube.)

6. Fill the chamber about half full with objects: stained glass fragments, beads, etc.

7. Dry solder the other hexagram to complete the chamber (see Photo 6). Then finish all seams, including the brass tube at the center.

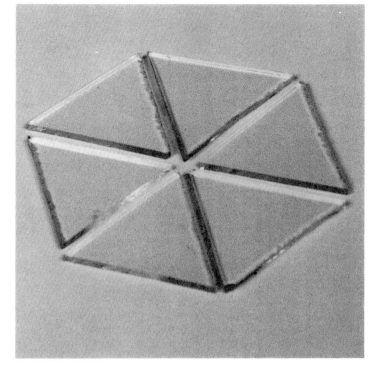

Photo 5

Photo 4

Photo 6

Examples of discs using stained glass techniques and sandwiched panes.

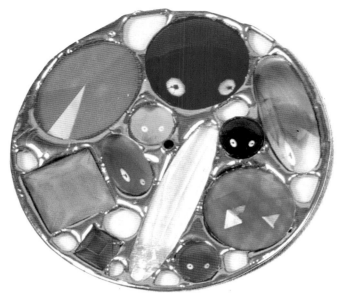

Discs

Discs can be constructed in many ways. For a stained glass disc, draw a 3" circle and divide it into segments. Choose your colors and textures. Cut the pieces using your pattern, leaving a 3/16" hole in the center to accommodate the brass eyelet (see Photo 7). Foil and join.

Discs can also be joined in this manner using faceted glass and plastic, agates and crystals. Explore other materials to incorporate.

You can sandwich objects (flowers, feathers, butterfly wings, etc.) between two panes of plexiglass. Tape the rims and drill a hole in the center.

Another technique involves casting objects in plastic resin in the form of a disc, which can be drilled with a hole in the center. Add the catalyst to some "casting resin," pour a layer into a round mold, lay your objects on top, pour the second layer, and let cure (see "Source Guide," and follow product directions).

Photo 7

Variations

The mirror configurations—hence body shape—can ve varied. Materials for the body can also vary, although using stained glass for the wheels is rather ideal. The body and the wheels can be ornamented with sculpted beads of solder.

The turning chamber can be mounted on an axis turned 90° so that objects are seen from the side, which would need to be clear. A three-dimensional wheel can also incorporate stained glass, crystals, globules, etc. on its surface rather than inside a chamber.

Turning object chambers can be interchangeable, each with different contents, or have a hinged door to empty and refill contents.

By constructing a hollow disc with plexiglass and epoxy, fluids of different densities and colors (mineral oils, glycerines, etc.) can be contained and viewed as they slowly swirl.

TAPERED SCOPE WITH SPHERES

ere's a contemporary variation on the parlor scope, featuring a unique mirror system that produces a three-dimensional, spherical image. This particular design uses marbles as viewing objects, to heighten the effect, but even a road map would look like a globe through these mirrors. And the eye piece at the top is so large you can see prismatic reflections of your eyes peering at the sphere from all angles.

Materials List

3 Stained glass panels: 1-3/4" x 4-3/4" x 8"

3 1st Surface mirrors: 1-1/8" x 3-7/8" x 7-3/4"

Clear glass triangle: 4-3/4" each side

Split ring (key ring): 1" diameter

Large playing marble ("bunker"): approx. 1"

1/8" Brass rod: 12" long

3 3/8" Brass balls with threaded holes (optional)

1. Cut the three stained glass panels. Clean and copper foil the edges. Solder them together (see "Construction Techniques") into a pyramid.

2. Cut the brass rod into thirds. Bend each one into a relaxed "V", to serve as legs. If you can't find the brass balls to screw into the legs as feet, hammer the ends into a tight curve.

3. Solder the three legs into the lower seams of the stained glass pyramid (as shown in Photo 1). Bend the legs as necessary to adjust the pyramid toward a balanced upright position.

Photo 2

Photo 3

Photo 1

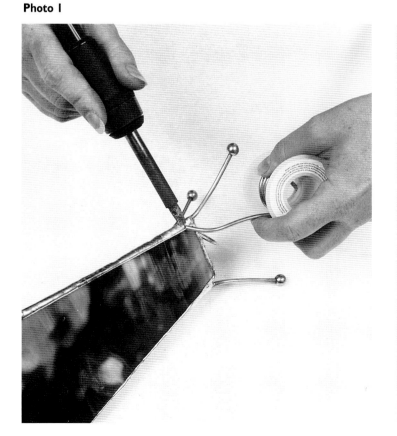

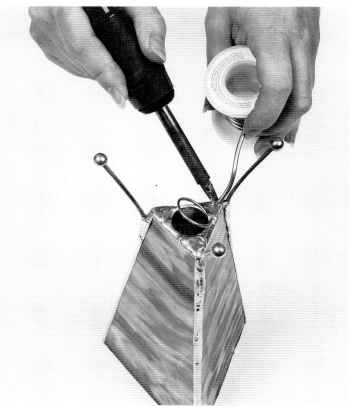

A close-up view of the spherical marble interior image (opposite).

Tapered scope with a variety of spheres which can be placed in or under the object chamber.

4. Pry open the split ring to about 40° to accommodate the marble with spring tension (see Photo 2).

5. Solder the split ring onto the legged end of the pyramid (see Photo 3). Clean off the flux, then fill in the gaps at the corners of the triangle with copper foil. Cover with solder, and clean off the flux again.

6. Cut and assemble the mirrors into a corresponding pyramid with duct tape. Add packing material (such as styrofoam sheets or felt) to the sides until the mirror assembly rests comfortably centered inside the stained glass pyramid (see Photo 4). Install the mirrors so that they fit snugly inside the body.

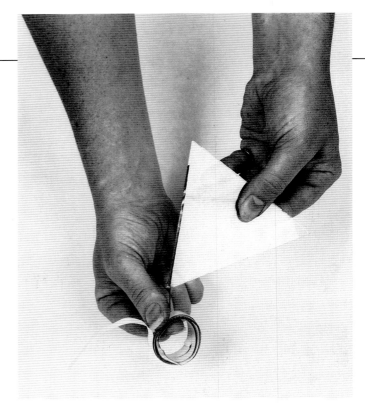

Photo 5

Photo 4

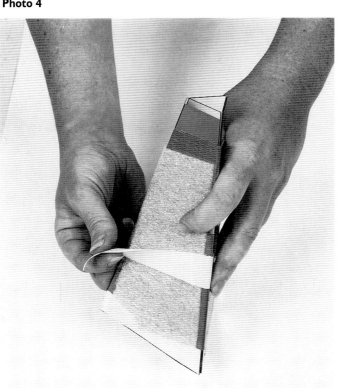

Photo 6

7. Foil the clear glass triangle (as shown in Photo 5). Coat with solder, clean, and dry solder the triangle onto the wide end of the stained glass pyramid, being careful to keep the mirrors clean as they are sealed.

8. Add copper foil to conform to the mirror opening. Flux and solder this margin around the viewing lens (as shown in Photo 6). Clean off flux.

9. Insert a marble into the split ring (see Photo 7). You can rotate the marble while viewing. You can also remove the marble, and place the scope over any image to view it, whether it is table-top or handheld.

Variations

If you are not inclined toward stained glass fabrication, you can still execute this design with other materials. Any kind of wood in 1/8" thickness would substitute nicely. Plastics and metals would also lend themselves appropriately.

The object end of the scope could be left unobstructed by a split ring and marble. This would allow for better viewing of other objects.

A major option of interest is the mirror system. This need not be a 3-mirror arrangement. A tapered 4-mirror system also produces a spherical image, but with different facets.

While maintaining similar proportions, the overall dimensions of this design can be altered up and down. Even teleidoscopic dimensions can be explored more fully.

A scope of this kind could be fitted with any number of object chambers: turning on different axes, interchangeable, fluid-filled, etc.

Photo 7

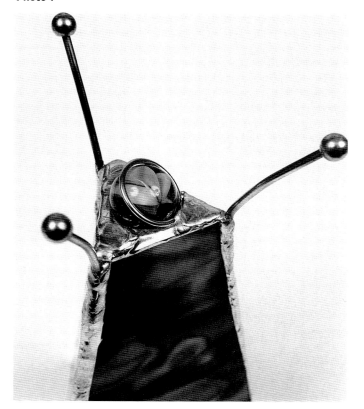

Interior view of turn-tray through a 3-mirror system.

SCARLET HILTIBIDAL

ANXIOUS

FIGHTING ANXIETY WITH
THE WORD OF GOD

Lifeway Press®
Nashville, Tennessee

Published by Lifeway Press® • © 2021 Scarlet Hiltibidal
Reprinted September 2021

No part of this book may be reproduced or transmitted in any form or by any means, electronic or mechanical, including photocopying and recording, or by any information storage or retrieval system, except as may be expressly permitted in writing by the publisher. Requests for permission should be addressed in writing to Lifeway Press®, One Lifeway Plaza, Nashville, TN 37234-0152.

ISBN: 978-1-0877-3386-9
Item: 005829921
Dewey decimal classification: 152.4
Subject heading: FEAR / ANXIETY / PEACE

To order additional copies of this resource, write Lifeway Resources Customer Service, One Lifeway Plaza; Nashville, TN, 37234-0113; FAX order to 615.251.5933; call toll-free 800.458.2772; email orderentry@lifeway.com; or order online at lifeway.com.

Printed in the United States of America

Lifeway Resources
One Lifeway Plaza
Nashville, TN 37234-0152

EDITORIAL TEAM,
LIFEWAY WOMEN
BIBLE STUDIES

Becky Loyd
Director, Lifeway
Women

Tina Boesch
Manager, Lifeway
Women Bible Studies

Sarah Doss
Team Leader, Lifeway
Women Bible Studies

Sarah Doss
Content Editor

Erin Franklin
Production Editor

Lauren Ervin
Graphic Designer

TABLE OF CONTENTS

DEDICATION

For Kaye Geiger, who led me through Bible studies on her living room floor, who discipled me without knowing it by letting me come through the unlocked garage door, and who helped me laugh and cry and pray and learn.

ABOUT THE AUTHOR

Scarlet Hiltibidal is the author of *Afraid of All the Things and He Numbered the Pores on My Face*. She writes regular columns for *ParentLife Magazine* and devotionals for *She Reads Truth* and enjoys speaking to women around the country about the freedom and rest available in Jesus. Scarlet has a degree in biblical counseling and taught elementary school before she started writing. She and her husband live in Southern California where she loves signing with her three daughters, eating nachos by herself, writing for her friends, and studying stand-up comedy with a passion that should be reserved for more important pursuits.

INTRODUCTION—
ANXIOUS TO BE HERE

I HAVE TOLD YOU

THESE THINGS SO THAT

IN ME YOU MAY HAVE

PEACE. YOU WILL HAVE

SUFFERING IN THIS WORLD.

BE COURAGEOUS! **I HAVE**

CONQUERED THE WORLD.

John 16:33

INTRODUCTION

We live in a broken, sad, scary place. There is plenty to be anxious about:

- dying;
- black holes;
- cancer;
- the fact that our phones have cameras on them that just sort of turn on sometimes;
- hurricanes;
- failing as a mom/friend/wife/employee/intermittent faster.

And the world is full of insufficient solutions for our anxiety:

- food;
- clothes;
- friends;
- medicine;
- hobbies;
- achievements;
- _____

Here's the thing. Nothing really works every-moment-all-the-time-perfectly-and-forever, right? Have you gotten to that point? That point where the counselor's advice just doesn't seem to stop the mind spiral quickly enough? Your closet is full of clothes, but your heart is still full of worry? You get the promotion, win the award, and achieve the goal, but instead of the peace it promises, you only find more fears? The bottom of the queso cup appears alarmingly fast, and you're left asking yourself, maybe out loud, *AM I JUST MORE MESSED UP THAN EVERYONE ELSE?*

I've been in that place so many times. I've been a slave to my panic, planning and avoiding and doing everything I could to insulate myself from pain and discomfort. But none of it worked.

So I made my life quiet. Isolated. "Under control."

I thought that would make me peaceful.

It didn't. Isolation and "control" might produce a quieter life, but peace isn't a quiet life; peace is a quiet soul. Peace is the gift of Jesus through the work of Jesus that we can have no matter what is going on in our living rooms or our in-boxes or our Instagram® feeds. The loudest of lives can't overwhelm the quiet that comes from Christ.

True peace comes when we learn to hold God's Word up to what worries us. There, we learn we can't fix ourselves; we can't protect ourselves. Instead, the Bible tells us we can rest, knowing Jesus walked into the broken, sad, scary place to rescue us and love us. He is the One who fixes. His is the only protection that matters.

When we fear the Lord rather than fearing the brokenness in our world, we can take hold of the perfect peace that is only available in Him.

The peace we are looking for is found in the already finished work of Christ (more on that later) revealed to us over and over again in God's Word, through prayer, and with our Christian community. When those of us who live with tornado awareness and constant cancer concern see the power of Jesus in the pages of the Bible, we can say with certainty, "The LORD is on my side; I will not fear. What can man do to me?" (Ps. 118:6, ESV).

WHERE ARE WE HEADED?

In this study, we'll look at different people in the Bible and what we can learn from them about anxiety. We'll discover how to live in freedom by clinging to God's Word and God's gospel in community and in prayer. This Bible study book will challenge you to study Scripture as you fight your worries. It will help you put some spiritual disciplines in place that will aid you in keeping your eyes on the cross of Christ (even if you've just seen an article show up on your Facebook® feed about the real-life dangers of black holes).

HOW DO I USE THIS STUDY?

This study is meant to be used in a small group setting. You are welcome to do this book on your own, but the study is designed to be done with others. Fighting anxiety alone is a lot like fighting an army alone. Imagine walking onto a battlefield by yourself while surrounded by enemies with bigger guns and stronger muscles. Actually, don't imagine that. This is supposed to help you with your anxiety, not add to it.

Every person should have her own Bible study book, a Bible, a pen, and some snacks.[1] In this book, you'll find personal study that you can do individually and a memory verse that you can learn on your own (and review together as a group). Also, flip to pages 186–187 in the Appendix to keep some of my favorite on-the-go, anxiety-blasting Scriptures handy! Then, when you come together, you'll watch a video and discuss your answers from the week's work as a group. **You'll find detailed information for how to access the teaching videos that accompany this study on the card inserted in the back of your book.**

During the final session of this study, we'll dive into what God's Word says about fighting anxiety together—why it is important and how the body of Christ is so vital in our approach to combating the lies anxiety tells us. I hope this study helps you as you engage with Scripture personally, and I hope you can use your personal study and experiences to encourage the other people in your group when you meet together.

So grab your five nearest neighbors. Or text your twelve closest coworkers. As a last resort, call your grandma and your sister and the lady that knows your order at the local Starbucks® and ask them to join you.

You'll find detailed information for how to access the teaching videos that accompany this study on the card inserted in the back of your Bible study book.

1. Snacks are not required but strongly recommended.

WHAT IF I NEED MORE THAN A BIBLE STUDY?

This study probably won't fix all your problems.

In 2004, Tim Keller preached a sermon called, "The Wounded Spirit." It had such an effect on me that I shared a good portion of it in the book I wrote about my personal fight with fear—*Afraid of All the Things*.

The thing is, I've been on anxiety pills. I've sat across from Christian psychiatrists while they offered big-word diagnoses to explain my particular version of anxiety.

I lived years feeling shame and fear over my mental weaknesses. I thought if my friends really knew how I struggled in my mind, they would reject me.

This sermon changed that for me. In it, Keller talked about different sources that might contribute to our woundedness and weakness. He didn't say, "Why are you so messed up? Just pray more!" He said, " . . . you know what the biblical answer is? It's complicated."[2]

That's what I want you to hear from me as you walk into this study. Your brain is complicated. Your anxiety could be rooted in an existential issue, or maybe for you, it's mostly physical. Maybe you have a bum thyroid. (I had mine taken out last year and the hormonal imbalance it causes can absolutely lead to anxiety and depression.) Maybe, as Proverbs 28:1 says, you flee "when no one pursues" (ESV) because you are intentionally walking in wickedness. In that case, a pill or a therapy session won't fix you like repentance will.

That's the driving message of Keller's sermon. There are many contributing factors. We must rely on prayer and God's Word, but we can do so while knowing that we might be dealing with physical sources or sin sources or emotional sources or existential (the BIG questions, like *What is life?*) sources. It's important to recognize these things as you fight your personal battle in your own personal way.

This study will not replace thyroid hormone medication or any other prescribed and necessary medication or weekly meetings with a Christian counselor or taking care of your health and well-being. Pursuing those outside resources, if and when needed, is wise and wonderful. Rather, this study is designed to help you, wherever you're at and whyever you're at it, to pursue Jesus in His Word, give you a better understanding of who He is, and learn how to set your mind on the things above (see Col. 3:2) and how to live your life consumed by the ultimate peace and joy of walking with Christ. If you find yourself needing a bit more support than this study offers, I encourage you to reach out to your local church or some trusted friends. I can look back on so many times in my own life that I needed help, and my Christian community, friends, and counselors definitely held me together during those times.

WILL IT ALWAYS BE THIS WAY?

About that "ultimate peace." I've never written from the stance of "I've overcome anxiety and so can you." If you're looking for ten easy steps, you won't find that here. In our broken world, it's a constant temptation to find a final fix. We hope to check the box and expect smooth sailing from then on. We will absolutely have smooth sailing someday. Just not in this world. The seas of this world have hurricanes. But the Lord has reminded me again and again, through His Word and His Spirit, that ultimate peace is our hope someday, but abundant life is available today.

Forever peace is coming, but present peace must be pursued.

We must learn to expect and accept the suffering Jesus promised us—"In this world you will have trouble . . ." (John 16:33, NIV)—all the while straining to see through all the sad and scary to the second half of the verse. There is Jesus, who tells us, " . . . take heart! I have overcome the world" (v. 33, NIV).

My hope is you'll walk into this study not looking for magic words that make fear disappear from your life forever but rather looking to and leaning on Jesus, who has already overcome everything that makes you anxious.

As you begin, give each member a Bible study book. Make sure to watch the video and go through the introductory material so everyone knows what to expect from this study. This week, you will complete the personal study for "Session Two: Anxious David." When you get back together next week, you will watch a video on Session Two and discuss your answers. As for this week, just watch the Session One video and use the discussion guide below to get to know one another.

WATCH

Write down any thoughts, verses, or things you want to remember as you watch the video for Session One of Anxious.

DISCUSS

Share names, family information, favorite restaurants, educational/vocational backgrounds, and current favorite things.

Do you struggle with anxiety? What does that battle look like in your life today?

Have you seen anxiety affect others in your community? Explain.

What are some ways you have tried to fight anxiety in the past? What helped? What didn't?

What are you hoping to take away from this study at the end of the eight weeks?

PRAY

As a group, take turns sharing prayer requests and figuring out how you want to pray for one another throughout the week. Maybe someone wants to take notes and send out a weekly email. Maybe you could all write your requests in a notebook. Find out what works for your group and make sure you have a way to touch base throughout the week. Close in prayer.

To access the teaching sessions, use the instructions in the back of your Bible study book.

NOTES

ANXIOUS DAVID

JESUS IS OUR SHIELD IN THE FIGHT AGAINST ANXIETY

MANY SAY ABOUT ME,

"THERE IS NO HELP FOR

HIM IN GOD." SELAH.

BUT YOU, LORD, ARE

A SHIELD AROUND ME,

MY GLORY, AND THE ONE

WHO LIFTS UP MY HEAD.

Psalm 3:2—3

DAY ONE
PRETEND INSANITY
1 Samuel 21:10–15 and Psalm 34

I have a lot of great conversations with myself while boiling water. When I'm doing tedious household things, my mind tends to wander to hypothetical relational problems. What if there's assigned seating at my step cousin's baby shower in two months, and what if her former roommate/friend is there and we're seated right next to each other, and what if she asks if our kids can get together for a playdate, which should be no big deal, and I guess the normal answer is "Sure!," but last time our kids got together, her kids taught my kids how to break into a car and start it with a bobby pin. So what am I going to say if she asks about that playdate? Maybe I just shouldn't go to the baby shower.

I'm exaggerating, but please tell me I'm not the only one who practices conversations for uncomfortable scenarios that don't actually exist yet.

Check one.

○ You're the only one who does this.

○ You too? This is exactly why I don't boil water.

It sounds crazy when I think about it, but that's what my brain does. Sometimes I'm afraid of people and the potential problems that come with people, and I think I can conversation-practice my way to peace. Let's see what David did when he was worried about potential relational conflict.

Read 1 Samuel 21:10-15. How did David act in the face of a threat to his safety? Write any observations in the space below.

Today, in 1 Samuel, we read about when David was so afraid of how King Achish might treat him that he pretended to be a crazy person. Pretty brilliant, right? It is amazing how our worries can lead us to behave. Maybe you tend to get tense and angry when you feel anxious about how others think about you or what they might say or do to you. Maybe you get defensive. Maybe you, like David, behave in ways that will scare people away. I mean, lion- and giant-slaying King David, of God's own heart, literally scribbled and drooled. Or maybe you isolate and put your phone on airplane mode so the texts and expectations can just stop for one minute, please!

How do you tend to struggle when it comes to relational anxiety?

Read Psalm 34.

Psalm 34 was actually written by David about this very time in his life—when he pretended to be a crazy person in the presence of Abimelech (probably the same guy mentioned earlier as "King Achish" in 1 Sam. 21:10-15).[1] David clearly knew what it was like to be anxious when he wrote this psalm.

Now let's focus on verses 1-4 of Psalm 34 for a second. How would you describe David's posture as he shared this message?

Sometimes, when I'm afraid, I forget how to pray. I forget how to think like a daughter of God. I panic and don't know what to say.

What do your prayers to the Lord sound like when you're stuck in a panic?

In verse 4, David said he "sought the LORD." Read the verse again and write what the Lord did as a result.

What do you think it means to seek the Lord?

What does verse 5 say is a result of looking to God?

When was the last time you felt joyful and void of shame? What was your relationship with God like at that time?

Read verse 8 from the CSB translation online. What emotion does the Bible say people who take refuge in God have?

On a scale of 1 to 10, how "happy" does your heart feel right now? (If you looked it up in a different translation, you may have seen the word *blessed*.) What do you think would move you closer to a 10?

|—— 1 —— 2 —— 3 —— 4 —— 5 —— 6 —— 7 —— 8 —— 9 —— 10 ——|

Not too happy.   The happiest.

Take the next few minutes to think about what it means to take refuge in the Lord. What are some things you find refuge in, apart from the Lord? What do you need to cut from your life or add to it to help you seek Him when you feel anxious?

In verse 11, David talked about teaching "the fear of the LORD." Fear is not a bad thing when it is focused on our Father. It's when we fear the wrong things that we feel anxiety.

What does God's Word say the fear of the Lord leads to? Look up the following verses and write the answer beside them.

Psalm 25:14

Psalm 33:8

Proverbs 9:10

Proverbs 14:26

Proverbs 14:27

Proverbs 19:23

Proverbs 22:4

Luke 1:50

When we fear the Lord, we gain. When we fear the Lord, it is easier not to worry about the things the Lord has already defeated. When we fear the Lord, we remember He is our shield and protector.

Read Psalm 34:9.

When we fear the Lord, what do we lack?

What are some misplaced fears you have right now? How does the work of Jesus impact those worries?

I'm not into war movies or battle-y things in general, but the idea of being shielded sounds awesome to me. If I could just be shielded, at all times, from danger, from conflict, from sadness—my heart longs for that. When I'm doing the boiling-water-conversing thing I told you about, what I'm really doing is trying to prepare and protect myself. David's interpersonal conflicts were much more murder-y than mine tend to be, but it's convicting and inspiring to me that he sought protection and refuge in the Lord.

Close out this time asking God to help you rest in the reality that He is eternally shielding you from the things that would harm your soul.

DAY TWO
DOEG IS NOT COOL

1 Samuel 22 and Psalm 27

I sat in a therapist's office last week and used my fifty allotted minutes to detail every relational conflict I could recall being involved in for the past fifteen years. My counselor wanted to know what my goal was—why I was seeking counseling and why I wanted to talk about closed-door conflicts from years past.

I said, "I feel haunted by my relational failures. I feel shame over the times I felt misunderstood. I just want to feel peace even though there are people from my past who might not think happy thoughts when they think of me."

Sometimes, I feel trapped by anxieties, stuck with thoughts of those I've been at odds with at one point or another. Maybe I've not had the same kinds of enemies, who carried swords and sought to kill, that David had, but I've had people who weren't for me. To one degree or another, we've all experienced enemies. It sure can feel like an enemy when things don't go as planned and you're walking through a divorce you never thought would happen, or when, yet again, an attempt to reconcile with an estranged family member ends in tears.

Enemies. No matter what form of conflict they bring to our lives, what do we do with them, and how can we find peace?

I'm really encouraged when I read about how David responded in prayer over his enemies. We're going to take a look at a psalm he wrote that theologian Charles Spurgeon thought was likely about a particular enemy of his named Doeg.[2] But first, let's get a little background on Doeg and how his life intersected with David's.

Read 1 Samuel 22 and answer the following:

What did Doeg tell Saul about what he witnessed between David and Ahimelech?

What did Saul command be done to Ahimelech and his priests for protecting David? Who carried out Saul's command?

Psalm 52 was written by David about the whole Doeg ordeal. It's definitely worth a read. But the Psalm I want you to open up to and focus on is Psalm 27. Though uncertain, Spurgeon believed David wrote this Psalm about Doeg as well.[3] And regardless of the motive, it is a powerful song for those of us who struggle with anxieties about enemies.

Read Psalm 27.

Write out the first phrase of each sentence in Psalm 27:1. Also, write out the two questions David posed in this verse.

David asked whom he should fear and whom he should dread, but he answered those questions even while asking them. What is the answer?

When the LORD is your light, salvation and stronghold, there is nothing else to fear. "LORD," or Jehovah, is the proper name of the one and only God of the universe. LORD means "The Existing One." "⁴ That means God doesn't just exist, but that He must exist. The LORD is the One from whom everything else that exists gets its existence. We may have enemies, but we also have the LORD. The ENT office receptionist who said you talked too fast, or the hurricane headed toward your coast, or even the hotdog you are scared to eat because your esophagus seems to be hotdog-shaped—everything and everyone is at the mercy of The Existing One. Your enemies are never more powerful than your LORD.

He is the stronghold of our lives. He is our light and our salvation. He is our source of true protection. We don't get to finish reading this page in this book without Him giving us the breath in our lungs, the sight in our eyes, and the clarity of our minds to do it.

What are some things/people/situations you sometimes fear rather than fearing the Lord?

Now back to Psalm 27. Reread verses 1-4. How do these verses help you get your mind off of your enemies and onto Jesus?

The Bible, the Old and New Testaments alike, are about the work of Jesus. When we read the first four verses of this psalm, as Christians living after the resurrection, we can see Jesus as the ultimate fulfillment of David's hope and the ultimate reason our enemies shouldn't cause anxieties. Through the work of Christ on the cross, we have received salvation forever. At the cross, our greatest enemies stumbled and fell. We can be confident, as David was, because we have a Jehovah who is also our Rescuer and proves our enemies are no match for Him. See "Becoming a Christian" on page 184 in the Appendix for more information about the Christian faith and how to commit to being a Christ-follower.

What was David wanting and asking of the Lord in verse 4?

What other verses can you think of that remind you that the God whose power dwarfs enemies like Doeg and Satan and everyone else is also whom we should most desire and whom we can most be satisfied in?

Our Lord, the conqueror of enemies, isn't just "The Existing One." He is our good Father and the giver of joy.

Copy the following verses below each of them:

For you did not receive a spirit of slavery to fall back into fear. Instead, you received the Spirit of adoption, by whom we cry out, "*Abba*, Father!"

ROMANS 8:15

You reveal the path of life to me; in your presence is abundant joy; at your right hand are eternal pleasures.

PSALM 16:11

When you're stuck worrying about your enemies, are you able to worship? If you can, get alone in this moment and sing God one of your favorite songs of praise.

If you don't feel like you can worship, and I know sometimes this happens to us, would you consider taking a moment to write an honest prayer to God below? Or reaching out to a trusted Christian friend with your struggle? God wants to know the truth of what's happening in your heart and mind and so does your faith family.

The last verse in Psalm 27 says, "Wait for the LORD; be strong, and let your heart be courageous. Wait for the LORD" (v. 14). The word wait, in the original Hebrew, means "to wait, look for, hope, expect."[5] When we look for, hope in, and expect our God to come through, we can be people of courage, even those of us (Hi!) who tend to lean more into worry.

What are some ways you can "Wait for the LORD" as you battle your fear of people?

God is able to shield us from pain because He went to the cross and took the pain. There is now no barrier between us. In Christ, there is a shield for us who trust Him. He is on our side. He is our defender. We don't need every human in the world to understand us when the God who made us and knows us—our best parts and the very worst ones—loves us that much.

At the end of the therapy session I mentioned earlier, my counselor helped me realize I was longing to tie up a bunch of loose, frayed ends in a world where not everything can have beauty and closure. Some things remain unfinished, unsaid, unheard, untied, unraveled. But see, we have a Shield. Not to protect us from all pain, but to protect us from pain that lasts forever. God is the only relational being who can love us perfectly and forgive us fully, and He does. The more I meditate on that, I know my eternity ends finished, tied, heard, and beautifully held together. Then it is easier for me to make peace with today's loose ends.

Close out this time asking the Lord to help you feel forever peace in a world that's lacking it.

DAY THREE
WHEN PRAYER TIME WAS THE WORST

Psalm 61

When I was nineteen, I was a hostess at a local restaurant known for its great salads. I started dating my husband who was a church planter/worship pastor and quickly left the great salad place to join the small church staff as the administrative assistant.

I'm embarrassed to admit this, but my least favorite part of our staff meetings was the prayer time.

Once a week, we'd all sit on the floor in our pastor's office and take turns praying. I'd listen to our pastor pray, then my husband, then the youth pastor, and, at that point, my heart would be beating out of my chest.

I hated prayer time.

Of course I understood the value of staff prayer. And of course I wanted to talk to God. But all I could think about while sitting in that little warehouse office space was what my words would show the other people in that office about how unspiritual I was. I wasn't in the prayer time to worship and to seek the Lord on behalf of the people we were serving together. I just hoped to say something that would garner a "Yes, Lord" or a nice, dramatic "Mmmm" from someone else in the room. I worried my prayers wouldn't seem potent enough for the people listening. But David modeled for us that prayer isn't something to worry about; rather, it is a weapon we can use against our worries.

Psalm 61 records one of David's prayers. It was definitely not the kind of prayer that might be said under duress in a church warehouse office space. David's prayer is earnest and needy and beautiful.

Scholars believe this psalm was written after David had come to the throne and was likely when his son, Absalom, was rebelling against him (which you can read about in 2 Sam. 15–18).[6] It was certainly a time when anxiety would be understandable.

Read Psalm 61:1-4 and reflect on David's tone with the Lord. Do you approach the Lord similarly?

When I read those first two verses, it struck me that David was pretty direct. He was so serious. He didn't say a bunch of words out of tradition or compulsion, as I did in the church office and still sometimes do today, but rather, he talked to God like he was talking to a real person.

Spurgeon noted that David's tone "was in terrible earnest." Then he said, "Pharisees may rest in their prayers; true believers are eager for an answer to them: ritualists may be satisfied when they have, 'said or sung' their litanies . . . but living children of God will never rest till their supplications have entered the ears of the Lord God of Sabaoth."[7]

Take a minute to read that over again. That convicted me so hard. I don't want to be a person who worriedly chants religious phrases in order to feel satisfied or make other people think I'm holy. I want to know and speak to the living God. Don't you?

Verse 2 says, "I call to you from the ends of the earth when my heart is without strength."

During seasons of anxiety or fear, we can approach the Lord in prayer and find Him to be a "refuge" and "rock" and "strong tower" as David described Him in verses 2-3. But anxiety often keeps us from that. It keeps us stuck in our own loop of fears—whether they are, *What will this church staff think of my prayer?* or *What will happen if my husband loses his job?* or *What is this lump under my arm?*

What's your first course of action when feeling anxious? Is it prayer? Is it TikTok®? Is it chips and queso?

Reread Psalm 61:4.

How do you think it helped David to pray this while dealing with exile?

Have you ever found comfort in your eternal destination while dealing with right-now suffering? What made that possible for you?

I just love verse 4. In fact, I think it is worthy of a nice "Mmmmmm." In that verse, we witness David doing the most wonderful and biblical thing, which I imagine crushed the anxiety he was facing. He, as Colossians 3:2 tells us to do, "set [his mind] on things above, not on earthly things."

In the following space, write down some right-now anxiety-inducing things in your life. And beside each one, find a Bible verse that helps you "Set your mind on things above" in regard to that struggle.

Now, read Psalm 61:5-8. Notice the change of tone.

Commentary writer Matthew Henry said, "David, in this psalm, as in many others, begins with a sad heart, but concludes with an air of pleasantness—begins with prayers and tears, but ends with songs of praise."[8]

That is so beautiful to me because I've experienced it. We can look at David's prayer in Psalm 61 and model our own anxious prayers after it. We can speak to the Lord directly and earnestly without pretense. We can set our minds on the eternal hope He offers, and we can conclude our prayers experiencing real peace, real hope, and real communion with the Father who loves us.

Below, write a prayer from your own heart and try to model it after Psalm 61. Be honest, reflect on eternity, and praise the Lord who is bigger than your worries!

DAY FOUR
CHASED AND HECKLED

2 Samuel 16:5–14 and Psalm 3

The heading for Psalm 3 in the CSB translation says, "Confidence in Troubled Times." When do you feel confident? Do you usually feel confident in "troubled times"?

My answer is certainly NO. When we lost our first baby in an ectopic pregnancy, I barely left my bed for months. When we adopted our middle daughter, who appeared to have significant physical and cognitive developmental delays, I barely left my bed for days. I've often buried myself under blankets in troubled times.

How do you usually react when times are troublesome?

Before we get any further, I want to say that making space to grieve is important. And we can turn toward God, even in our grief. He wants to sit with us in it, to carry us in it. All clear? Great. Back to Psalm 3.

The Bible tells us this was "A psalm of David when he fled from his son Absalom." You may remember from yesterday's study that this is the same time period scholars believe David penned Psalm 61.[9]

The events that led to the writing of this psalm are found in 2 Samuel 15–18 when David was betrayed by Absalom and others in his life. Absalom was leading a rebellion against his dad, the king. People who were at one time his friends turned against him. It was an undoubtedly troubled time in the life of David. It was, what some theologians might call, a "where's my blanket" moment.

Read 2 Samuel 16:5-14. Now, let's look more closely at verses 5-8. Who was Shimei, and what was he doing?

Read verses 11 and 12 again. What emotion do you pick up on from David? How did his response reflect a trust in the God of justice?

In verses 13 and 14, David moved on down the road, going his way while Shimei went on cursing him. Then it says, David "refreshed himself" (v. 14, ESV). It's really crazy to me that David was able to experience peace given his circumstances. Remember—he was on the run from his own son! His son, who should have been in his corner. And then, he was being heckled by this Shimei guy. And somehow, "he refreshed himself." There's no way unless God was helping him, right?

Now, flip to Psalm 3 and read the whole chapter. Take a closer look at verses 1 and 2.

I wonder if his "refreshing himself" was similar to the prayer we find in Psalm 3?

In Psalm 3:3, David called God his shield, his glory, and the lifter of his head. Below, next to these powerful names for God, explain how these terms were refreshing for David in his time of trouble and how they might be of help to you.

SHIELD	
GLORY	
LIFTER OF MY HEAD	

God is our protector (shield). Nothing can get to us without first getting through God. God is our source of significance (glory). We can fight anxiety knowing the things we worry about could never truly jeopardize the value we have because we are approved by God through Jesus. God is the lifter of our heads. God is the one who leads us to look up from our sorrows and worries and reminds us we can have joy and hope through our friendship with Him.

Which of these three descriptions of God's work in our lives means the most to you right now? Why?

Take another look at verses 5-6.

In these verses, David slept. It can be hard to sleep when you feel anxious (even if you rarely leave your bed). I love the idea of praying psalms like this one when your mind and body aren't cooperating.

Revisiting verses 7-8, what words or phrases show that God is for you in these verses?

How do you need God to fight for you right now as you battle anxiety and troubled times?

Close your time today thanking God for saving you and blessing you. Thank Him for rising up, in Jesus, to strike the enemies of sin and death and failure and fear. You belong to Him, and He has overcome. Ask Him to help you see Him as your shield, glory, and hope. Ask Him to help you sleep and not be afraid.

DAY FIVE
SHEPHERD AND SHIELD

Psalm 23

In Psalm 23:1, David wrote, "The LORD is my shepherd; I have what I need."

I have what I need. What if we really believed that?

Oftentimes when I'm anxious, my worry is rooted in feeling like I'm lacking something. My mind tells me, *If I just had this . . . or If that circumstance would just line up the right way . . . THEN, I'd have what I need.*

What is it, right now, that your mind is telling you that you need to have peace?

Read Psalm 23.

Look at verse 2 and highlight the phrase "he leads."

I heard an illustration from Elisabeth Elliot about Psalm 23 in which she talked about getting lost in the car and needing directions. Updating her example a little, imagine using your iPhone GPS to get somewhere, but then, while you are traveling, your phone dies, and you don't have your charger.

Maybe you pull over and ask someone how to get to where you're going, and he/she starts giving you a long, detailed, confusing explanation. But then imagine how you would exhale if someone were to simply drive ahead of you and lead the way. Elliot said, " . . . isn't it a relief if somebody just says, 'Follow me.'"[10]

There's no doubt that an anxious mind complicates a simple thing. Sure, we've all got complicated, painful relationships. Sure, we're juggling lots of responsibilities and wearing lots of hats and dealing with lots of incoming problems. And of course, you, if you were really smart, might be building a tornado shelter right now. But let's just remember this truest of true things. We are sheep, and we have a Good Shepherd who loves us and who leads us.

Read the following verses and write down the phrase Jesus kept saying to His people: Matthew 16:24; Mark 1:17; Mark 10:21; Luke 5:27.

When we think about the role of a shepherd, we remember that a shepherd takes care of his sheep, provides for them, leads them, and protects them.

What are some examples from your own life of when your Good Shepherd has taken care of, provided, led, and/or protected you?

Psalm 23:4 in the CSB translation uses the phrase, "darkest valley," but I love the imagery used in the ESV translation—"valley of the shadow of death." I used to think of that phrase as reflective of the very worst horrors life has to offer—things like disease and abuse. But, truly, this whole life is the "valley of the shadow of death," right? We are all dying every day. Some days are filled with pleasantries, and some days are filled with pain, but we live every moment in the shadow of death.

Even though we are all walking toward death, we can "fear no evil" (v. 4, ESV). Why?

Verse 6 refers to the day we will dwell in the house of the Lord. Is there a home you love to visit? Maybe it is your childhood home? Or maybe your own childhood home was filled with dysfunction, but every time you visited that one aunt or grandma or that one friend, you were met with warmth and food and comfort and love?

Describe that setting in the space below.

All week, we've been looking at David. There's so much of his life we didn't have time to cover. Have you ever heard about the time he was a scrawny young boy who slayed the giant, Goliath, with a sling, some stones, and without physical armor (1 Sam. 17)? Or, you know, that time he sinned against Bathsheba and then had her husband killed (2 Sam. 11–12)? I mean . . . David lived a *life*.

He had lots of great days and lots of bad ones. Based on his life events, he likely experienced the anxiety of being the victim and the anxiety of being the bad guy. But he was a bad guy with faith in a good God. He was often a bad guy whose prayer life demonstrated that he sought forgiveness and protection, not through an earthly shield (not even when fighting a giant) but an eternal One. God protected David from his fears and from following his sin to destruction. God guarded and guided His child through all kinds of circumstances we can hardly imagine.

Now skip over to the New Testament and read about when God, the Good Shepherd, was walking the earth in flesh. Read John 10:1–11. What did Jesus call Himself in verse 7?

What did Jesus call Himself in verse 11?

Look at Psalm 23 and read through it again, but every time you see the phrases "the LORD" or "He," say, "Jesus."

Jesus is my shepherd;
I have what I need.
Jesus lets me lie down in green pastures;
Jesus leads me beside quiet waters.
Jesus renews my life;
Jesus leads me along the right paths
for his name's sake.
Even when I go through the darkest valley,
I fear no danger,
for Jesus is with me;
Jesus' rod and his staff—they comfort me.

Jesus prepares a table before me
in the presence of my enemies;
Jesus anoints my head with oil;
my cup overflows.
Only goodness and faithful love will pursue me
all the days of my life,
and I will dwell in the house of Jesus
as long as I live.

Here's the thing. Because of Jesus, we have access to the Shepherd. Because of Jesus, we have access to safety and satisfaction. Because of Jesus, we are sheep who don't need to be afraid of the lingering wolves in our lives. He leads us. He loves us. He is with us.

We are like David in that we fail, but Jesus doesn't. We worry, but Jesus understands. Jesus knows this world is broken, sad, and scary. But when we hold up what we are anxious about next to the good news of the gospel, we see that we actually can rest because He has already handled everything on our behalf. We are His, and He has won, is winning, and will win forever. It's not a onetime thing. It's an everyday opportunity to sit at His feet and in His Word, to claim His promises, think on His help, and believe in His power.

What can you do this week to remember the truth—that Jesus, your Shepherd, is with you—loving you, comforting you, leading you, holding you, and protecting you?

This past week, you completed the Session Two personal study in your books. If you weren't able to do so, no big deal! You can still follow along with the questions, be involved in the discussion, and watch the video. When you are ready to begin, open up your time in prayer and push play on Video Two for Session Two.

WATCH

Write down any thoughts, verses, or things you want to remember as you watch the video for Session Two of Anxious.

FROM THIS WEEK'S STUDY

As a group, review this week's memory verse.

Many say about me,
"There is no help for him in God." *Selah.*
But you, LORD, are a shield around me,
my glory, and the one who lifts up my head.

PSALM 3:2-3

REVIEW SESSION TWO PERSONAL STUDY

From Day One: In Psalm 34:11, David talked about teaching "the fear of the LORD." What are some things we learned that the fear of the Lord leads to (include your favorite references from the chart on p. 21)?

From Day Two: Which Bible verses remind you that the God whose power dwarfs enemies like Doeg and Satan and everyone else is also whom we should most desire and whom we can be most satisfied in?

From Day Three: Do you approach the Lord similarly to the way David did in Psalm 61:1-4?

What's your first course of action when feeling anxious? Is it prayer? Is it TikTok®? Is it chips and queso?

From Day Four: Which of these three descriptions of God's work in our lives means the most to you right now? Why?

From Day Five: What are some examples from your own life of when your Good Shepherd has taken care of, provided, led, and/or protected you?

DISCUSS

What is the most interesting thing you worried about this week? :)

What have we learned about who God is through our look at some of the anxiety-inducing events in David's life?

How have David's prayers helped you?

When David was fleeing from Absalom, he prayed, "But you, LORD, are a shield around me" (Ps. 3:3a). Share about a time in your life when the Lord was your shield.

Back in Day One, we looked at verses all over the Bible that show us what happens when we fear the Lord. Which of these benefits resonates with you? If you're comfortable doing so, share a testimony of that experience in your group.

PRAY

Take turns sharing anxieties you're dealing with right now and have your group talk about how the gospel speaks to those worries. Spend the remainder of your time in prayer for each other.

To access the teaching sessions, use the instructions in the back of your Bible study book.

ANXIOUS JONAH

JESUS IS OUR KING IN
THE FIGHT AGAINST ANXIETY

BUT SEEK FIRST THE

KINGDOM OF GOD AND

HIS RIGHTEOUSNESS, AND

ALL THESE THINGS WILL

BE PROVIDED FOR YOU.

THEREFORE **DON'T WORRY**

ABOUT TOMORROW,

BECAUSE TOMORROW WILL

WORRY ABOUT ITSELF.

EACH DAY HAS ENOUGH

TROUBLE OF ITS OWN.

Matthew 6:33—34

DAY ONE
RUN!

Jonah 1

I grew up in a time of old. In a time before GPS was a thing. A time when one could get "lost" in the city she lived in and have to drive around until something looked familiar.

Terrifying, I know.

The absolute worst was when I'd be riding in the backseat of the car with my mom behind the wheel and I'd see her shoulders tense up and hear her mumble, "We're lost . . . and this . . . is . . . a bad . . . neighborhood."

I was very aware of "bad neighborhoods" and all that they entailed because my adoptive dad worked the night shift as a SWAT cop/helicopter pilot in Miami-Dade. We were, at the time, the second most crime-ridden county in America. I know these things, because of course I do. So, as you might imagine, his answers to, "How was work last night, Daddy?" were . . . intense.

I remember regularly sliding out of my seatbelt and becoming one with the floorboard of the car. My large fear of being killed by bad guys overpowered my medium fear of dying in a car accident without a seatbelt on.

So I definitely identify with Jonah and his caution/fear/aversion/panic over "bad neighborhoods" and the "bad people" there. I identify with running away from a scary place. Let's look at his situation in the Book of Jonah.

Read Jonah 1.

Now, take a look at verses 1-3.

What did God tell Jonah to do?

How did Jonah respond?

Here's what you need to know about Jonah and Nineveh. Jonah was an Israelite. Nineveh was the capital of Assyria, which was Israel's worst enemy. One thing commentators say that made them so scary was that the Ninevites had an established reputation for treating their enemies badly.[1]

In other words, Jonah's fear was warranted. It would be like if you'd asked me, during my one-with-the-floorboard moment, to go for a nice jog by myself on the same street where my dad had been shot at by murderous drug lords during his last shift. Jonah's fear was rational, but that didn't mean he couldn't be obedient.

Can you think of a time in your life when you "pulled a Jonah" and did the exact opposite of the thing you felt the Spirit prompting you to do because you were scared?

Read Jonah 1:4-17.

How did God respond to Jonah's disobedience?

In *The NIV Application Commentary*, James Bruckner, reflecting on Jonah telling the men of the boat to throw him overboard, wrote, "The captain hopes what Jonah already knows, that his God is compassionate."[2]

And then, as the story goes on, we see God's creative and perfectly timed compassion in the form of a big fish.

In verse 17, Jonah was eaten by a fish. I used to think of this part of the story as a punishment because . . . gross. But what mercy! God was saving Jonah's life. A big fish and a dark place brought a second chance.

Can you think of a time in your own life when God gave you a fresh opportunity or a second chance? Describe it below.

Maybe you grew up in church and the whole fish-eating-a-man-and-man-surviving thing sounds totally normal to you. But maybe you're more like, *This is the weirdest, most ridiculous religious story ever.*

If you're more in that second camp, I found this really fascinating. Have you ever heard of *Encyclopedia Britannica*? Well, apparently, if you were to reach out to them to request research about Jonah being swallowed by a whale, they would send you information that not only scientifically proves the possibility that a man could be swallowed and survive in a whale, but they'd include an actual article about an event that transpired in 1891. A large sperm whale swallowed a sailor named James Bartley. In time the whale was captured, and his stomach was opened the next day. The sailor was found in the stomach, unconscious, but alive. He survived.[3]

Good luck ever going in the ocean again, but I love that God allowed that to happen. What a horrible few days for that dude, but what a helpful story for skeptics. God is supernatural, working within this natural world He created, and He reaches in and rescues again and again, creatively and redemptively.

This week, we're talking about Jonah and how Jesus is our King in the fight against anxiety. Often, in my life, my fears are king. My doubts are king. But it is so huge to remember the power of the real King.

God didn't just make a giant fish swallow Jonah; He made the giant fish. Out of nothing. And He didn't just make the giant fish in the vast ocean; He made the vast ocean. The King of your heart can make worlds and move whales to help His kids take the right next step.

What is a next right step of obedience for you? What is something you've sensed the Spirit leading you to?

Read Jonah 1:17 again.

"The LORD appointed" can be such a comfort.

What is the situation you fear most right now?

How would you ask God to help if you really believed He's an ocean-making, whale-moving King?

Close this day out reflecting on ways you've seen God's hand in situations in which you were initially scared. Or write out a prayer asking the Lord to help you respond to the circumstances you face with faith instead of fear.

DAY TWO
STUCK IN A FISH

Jonah 2 and Romans 8:26–30

For several years in my young adulthood, I lived as a slave to a secret eating disorder. My food dysfunctions and the lengths I took to hide them completely ruled me. My anxiety surrounding my big secret was crushing. See, I wasn't just a person. I wasn't just a Christian. I was a church secretary. I was a young pastor's wife. I was a Bible college student. I was all these very super-Christian-y things, and I was certain that if I came clean about my sins, I'd lose everything.

So I fought in secret. I prayed and cried and quietly begged God for healing. My prayers didn't seem to go far though, and it was because my heart was full of pride. I was unwilling to be obedient to the Spirit's leading. My sin was the king in my life, and as much as I wanted to worship the real King, I felt like my fears kept me stuck. God kept bringing me to Proverbs 28:13—"The one who conceals his sins will not prosper, but whoever confesses and renounces them will find mercy."

But I was too afraid. I was afraid that if I obeyed, if I confessed, I would lose everything. I thought I'd destroy my reputation. I thought my husband would leave me. I thought my family would be disgusted and disown me.

What fears do you have that keep you from obedience when you encounter a command in God's Word or direction from the Holy Spirit?

My worries kept me stuck in sinful patterns for three-and-a-half years. But when I finally confessed my sin to others, God took my one, weak moment of obedience, and He healed me. My desire to be dysfunctional with food evaporated, and I never struggled with it again. It was maybe the most miraculous thing I've ever experienced.

The disclaimer I always give when I tell this story is that there are things I've been praying for my entire life that are still unresolved. I know God doesn't always give miraculous overnight healing, but sometimes He does. Jonah and I have that in common. God is capable of orchestrating major, miraculous deliveries.

Do you have a story like mine? A time you hit rock bottom/the end of yourself and felt stuck in something you couldn't get out of? Did you run to the Lord for help or run from Him? Share a little bit about your experience below.

Commentator James Montgomery Boice said the following about this point in Jonah's story:

To concentrate so much on what happened inside the great fish that we miss noting what happened inside Jonah is to make a great mistake . . . So we must now turn to Jonah's prayer to God from inside the monster. As we read it we discover that the prayer reveals the truly great miracle. It shows that though Jonah had been brought to the depths of misery within the fish, he nevertheless found the mercy of God in his misery. He discovered that though he had forsaken God, God had not forsaken him, though it seemed that he had. In brief, Jonah found salvation even before the fish vomited him up on the land.[4]

Chills, right?

A human heart receiving God's mercy is a miracle.

Jonah didn't pray magic words that bought him a second chance. His heart shifted. His fear stopped ruling his actions, and he spoke to God with humility and desperation. That's a miracle.

In the space below, write about a time in your faith life when you experienced the miracle of a heart shift—an upward posturing—a moment when you stopped pursuing self and started pursuing the Savior. If you have never experienced anything like this, write about what you feel is holding you back. Is it fear? Is it pride? Is it a desire to hold onto control?

Read Jonah 2.

Until studying this passage, I never realized that Jonah's recorded prayer is referencing an earlier prayer. From the belly of the big fish, in verse 2a, he said, "I called out to the LORD, out of my distress, and he answered me . . ." (ESV) referring to whatever prayer of desperation he prayed when he was thrown overboard, facing death.

Here's what's cool to me. There's no way that in that moment, as he was flung from the boat into the storm, Jonah said a thoughtfully worded and perfectly crafted petition to the God who was in control of the storm. I wonder if his prayer was a simple "AHHHHHHHH!" or "Heeeeeeelp meeeee!" or "GOOOOOOOOOD!"

In some of my lowest moments, my prayers were less about words and more about desperation. One of the countless beautiful mysteries about the Holy Spirit is that when He lives in you, He intercedes for you. He helps you pray when you don't know what to say.

Read Romans 8:26-30.

How are you weak right now?

In light of your weakness, what do you think the Spirit might pray on your behalf?

In just that small Romans passage we not only have the Holy Spirit interceding for us but also the Father working all things for our good and the Son showing us how to live in the promise of being justified and glorified.

Whether you are alone on your couch right now or being flung over the railing of a storm-shaken ship, you have an incredible King in the fight against anxiety. You have a King who prays for you even as He promises you He'll make sure you win.

Look back at Jonah 2, specifically verse 9. What do we see as part of Jonah's prayer here?

I'm going to tell you the answer. ☺ It's gratitude. I've heard it said that thanksgiving is the remedy to anxiety. It's hard to be scared when you know why you're grateful. Remember the miracle of God's mercy and surrender your worry.

In the space below, write out a prayer of thanksgiving and ask God to deliver you from what you're anxious about today or help you give up whatever might be holding you back from following the Holy Spirit's leading in your life.

DAY THREE
BIG CITIES AND SACKCLOTH AND MOST LIKELY TO BE MUGGED
Jonah 3; Luke 11:11-13 and John 3:16

I presently (and since the beginning of time) get anxious when visiting big cities. *Will I be able to figure out how and where to park? Will I get mugged? Probably most carjackings happen in big cities, right? If I survive the attempted muggings and jackings, will I remember where I parked?*

At this point, we've already established that God was sending Jonah to a place called Nineveh and that there were scary people there. And, guess what, there are still scary people there. Nineveh is now called Mosul, Iraq, which might be the number one country you don't want to visit if you're a Christian. In 2019, the *BBC* put out an article titled "Iraq's Christians 'close to extinction.'"[5]

Thinking about such dangers helps me have compassion for Jonah when reading his story. Jonah went to a big city with scary, violent people because God asked him to go.

I know this is scary to write out on paper, but what is a place you would have a hard time being willing to go to if you felt God leading you there? Why?

I've always hated questions like the one I just asked. Some broken part of me sometimes forgets the kindness of God and assumes He is out to get me.

Like, I better not tell God what I don't want to do because then He will for sure make me do it.

Does your head ever sound like that?
○ Yes
○ No

Read Luke 11:11-13. To worry God is out to get us is to forget what kind of Father He is. List some of the "good gifts" God has given you in the space below.

Now let's look at Jonah 3. Perhaps the craziest part of this story is that when Jonah finally did go visit his literal worst, most violent enemies, they actually listened.

Read Jonah 3:5-10. How did the people of Nineveh respond to Jonah's message, and what did God do?

In ancient times, fasting and wearing sackcloth was a sign of mourning. Verse 5 begins by saying the Ninevites "believed God." The fasting and wearing of rough, goat-hair clothing was a response to their recognition of sin. They mourned their sin. Belief came first. Followed by repentance. Followed by the mercy of God. It's so amazing and simple, but this is another way worriers can get it wrong. It can actually be frustrating and scary to read an instance like that.

My brain, for instance, can easily read chapter 3 and think, *But how do I perfectly posture my heart? How do I ensure my repentance is enough? Is sackcloth Prime® eligible?*

However, it should be so much easier for us to repent and rejoice and rest in the forgiveness of God than it was for the Ninevites. We don't just have the message of Jonah; we have the actions of Jesus.

Read John 3:16 (or just recite it to yourself).

Now underline, circle, highlight, or burn this next sentence into your brain—Jesus is enough.

Jesus' perfection, not your sin, His sacrifice on the cross, not your sackcloth, His power, not your weakness, is what God sees and approves and why God loves without stopping and forgives without going back.

When we get so caught up in "our part," that's where the anxiety kicks in. As the old hymn says,

Turn your eyes upon Jesus,
Look full in His wonderful face,
And the things of earth will grow strangely dim,
In the light of His glory and grace.[6]

Inside the following graphic, make a list of "I believe . . ." statements about God and back them up with Scripture references. Here are some places to look:

ROMANS 6:22	2 CORINTHIANS 3:17	EPHESIANS 2:8–9
2 TIMOTHY 1:7	1 PETER 2:16	1 JOHN 1:9

I BELIEVE . . . For example, I believe that nothing can separate me from the love of God (Rom. 8:38-39).

Here's the thing. When we believe in the goodness of God, we won't care as much where He asks us to go. When we remember we too were the Ninevites and God responded to our repentance with grace and more grace, we can worry less about the cities we hope to never see or the fact that we've never owned sackcloth. The King who leads us loves us.

He wants us to have a vibrant, ever-growing relationship with Him. He wants us to experience the joy of trusting and obeying.

In the space below, write out a prayer. Ask the Lord to set you on a mission that helps you grow more and more aware that He is on the throne, that He is good, and that your anxieties don't have the power to rule over you.

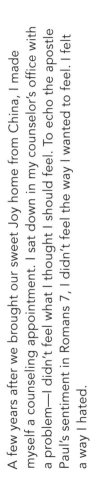

DAY FOUR
WHEN PREFERRING DEATH

Jonah 4

A few years after we brought our sweet Joy home from China, I made myself a counseling appointment. I sat down in my counselor's office with a problem—I didn't feel what I thought I should feel. To echo the apostle Paul's sentiment in Romans 7, I didn't feel the way I wanted to feel. I felt a way I hated.

I wanted love to be the cure-all in our adoption story. I wanted the bonding to happen more quickly—instantaneously, even. I mean, aren't Christians supposed to come chock-full of supernatural love for others? How could I, new mother of this miracle, feel anything other than awe and gratitude? Why was I so easily frustrated with our child—a former orphan—when she didn't behave correctly or even when she couldn't do things easily? What kind of monster feels anything but compassion and affection for a child with disabilities?

I bring this up because, if reading Jonah 4 through the lens of my old, pious church-lady self, I'd be like, Hang on. Jonah just got a second shot at loving his enemies—and they actually listened? And they turned to the Lord? Mission accomplished. Jonah was safe. Um . . . why does chapter four start the way it does?!

I'm getting ahead of myself, aren't I?

Go ahead and read Jonah 4.

How does verse 1 tell us Jonah felt on the heels of all the great stuff God had just used him to do?

Do you, at all, resonate with Jonah here? Can you think of a time you knew how you ought to act/feel/believe but found yourself in the wrong?

If you're honest, I think you have to say yes. We long to be in control—little gods of our own universe—making the plans and calling the shots. Jonah was so angry that God had mercy on the evil Ninevites that he literally asked God to let him die (v. 3). Wow.

What is the last thing Jonah is recorded to have said in the Bible book named after him (v. 9b)?

Those are some pretty intense last words for a book of the Bible. It was not Jonah's best moment. Probably not the words he'd want on his gravestone, or, I don't know, at the very end of his titular book in the HOLY SCRIPTURES.

But here's what's cool. Jonah is not the hero of this book.

Even the WHALE, the accurately vomiting rescuer, is not the hero of this book. Author and Bible teacher Priscilla Shirer said it like this, "These four little simple chapters are not really about the whale; they're about our God."[7]

Read Jonah 4:10-11. What does the end of this book tell you about God?

There is so much to learn from Jonah's story. We learn that God is gracious and slow to anger. We learn that God's plan is redemption when our plan might be revenge. Jonah reacted wrongly to seeing God spend His mercy on the people of Nineveh, the same mercy that had saved Jonah again and again. He could have been moved and grateful for the compassion of God in His own life and the compassion of God for his enemies. But he wound up bitter and miserable.

Two things I don't want us to pass by here: 1. Jonah missed out on the joy he could have experienced being used by God in the redemption of the Ninevites. 2. Even when Jonah was feeling angry and hopeless, God continually tried to engage with him. God didn't leave him alone in his bad attitude. And God does the same for us. He engages our hearts, even when our hearts are hard.

When you look at the circumstances and struggles in your own life, do you focus on the role others play? Do you focus on your own part? Or do you look for God? Do you look for the hope—the healing, the redemption, the restoration project—that Jesus is working on?

In the space below, list out some of the circumstances you're currently struggling to sort out. Where is God? What do you think your King is doing?

I don't have the full picture, but I can already see so much of God's presence and power in the story of Joy and this adoptive family He's put her into. When I struggled to feel the right things, I was comforted by another adoptive mom who shared she'd felt the same things too. When God allowed us to walk through various medical issues with Joy, I was astounded by how He used those situations to bring us closer together as a family. I don't get how the whole thing works, guys. But I know God blesses us with the most amazing gifts. Gifts like healing. Gifts like growth. Gifts like the ability to lay our heads down at night without feeling the weight of our burdens. Gifts like having hearts that are able to say, "God, this hurts, but thank You for it." God knows how to love as He leads.

DAY FIVE
JONAH, NINEVEH, AND YOU!

Matthew 6:25-34 and Matthew 12:38-41

Last night, I had a dream about recording the videos for this Bible study. Brace yourself, because I know nothing is more riveting, interesting, and helpful than hearing the details of someone's super weird dream. ☺

So it was the first day of shooting the videos for this study (about fighting anxiety with the Word of God). In my dream, I got to the set, and everything I was wearing or had brought to change into was stained, pilling, and had huge holes in it. Then, the producer walked up and said, "Scarlet, we want you to wear this Anna costume—so you'll be dressing like the princess from Frozen® while you teach the Bible, OK?" And then I nodded and stepped into the changing room to learn that the costume was sized for a toddler. It was all a tragedy.

This just goes to show you where my mind was. *HOW CAN I TEACH A BIBLE STUDY WITHOUT THE RIGHT OUTFIT ON!?*

OK. Now, make me feel better by answering this next question, please.

When is the last time you fixated on a super non-important aspect while preparing for an important thing?

What was important in that situation and what were you focused on instead?

It's really sad that Jonah, even after failing to obey God in his fear, even after his second chance, even after obeying and being used by God in such a clear way, lost focus. Jonah was essentially the toddler-sized-Anna-costume wearer of the Old Testament. Throughout this story, we see an anxious and cowardly Jonah turn into an angry and bitter Jonah, but all throughout the story, his eyes were on the wrong prize.

Both anxiety and anger usually reveal a heart that is focused on the wrong things.

So what are we to do? We're often anxious, angry, bitter, and resentful, aren't we? Or we are too busy stuffing our faces or our Amazon® carts to notice we are. So what's the cure? Who is our hope? How can we have peace and be people who are consumed by love instead of fear? How can we avoid an ending like Jonah's?

It's certainly not by trying harder and doing better and faking it till we're making it.

Let's read Matthew 6:25-34. What does the heading in your Bible say right before verse 25? If your Bible doesn't have a heading, what do you think the heading could be?

Looking at my version, the CSB (Christian Standard Bible), it says, "The Cure for Anxiety." Before you continue reading Jesus' living words in Matthew 6, I want you to pray that the Spirit will remove any cynicism or disbelief that leads you to think there's not real hope. Jesus says there is. Let's believe Him.

Now look at verse 25. Would you agree that "life [is] more than food and the body [is] more than clothing"? Why or why not?

It's easier to agree to than it is to believe. Maybe you agree life is more than food and clothing, but your actions say otherwise. Maybe you followed God to Nineveh, but your emotions don't line up with your mission. Maybe your focus is on shaky things because your heart is doubting what is solid.

So what's at the root of our anxiety? The *ESV Study Bible* says, "To be anxious . . . demonstrates a lack of trust in God, who promises that he will graciously care for 'all these things.'"[8]

Read verses 26-34. Jesus told us to consider the birds and the flowers. What else can we consider, not listed in this passage, that Jesus cares for and sustains? List as many things as you can in the space below.

We see Jesus here, in His infamous Sermon on the Mount, telling us why we're anxious. We worry about food and clothes and video shoots and getting even and getting rewarded, and it all boils down to ME-ME-ME-ME-ME-ME!

So what do we do? Copy Matthew 6:33 in the space below.

What does "all these things" refer to?

"All these things" are the things we chase. Food. Clothing. Status. Security. The secret is that it's only when we pursue the King that we find our needs and, more importantly, our souls satisfied.

Jesus is our King in the fight against anxiety. He has to be.

Read Matthew 12:38-41. Even sinful, anxious, bitter Jonah was used by God. List some of the ways God used him to point people to Himself.

The most important thing about Jonah is that he points us to Jesus. "Something greater than Jonah is here" (v. 41). Thank God! Jonah knew how to preach repentance, but then he whined when it worked. Jesus preaches repentance, but then when we turn and call on His name, He forgives. Guys, Jesus forgives us! He forgives us when we're too anxious to obey. He forgives us when we obey with poor motives. He forgives us when we lose focus and fail to trust Him and make our fears our temporary king. King Jesus can take care of us. King Jesus is going to take care of us.

Do you meditate on this reality? Do you preach the good news of Christ's death and resurrection to your heart when you're feeling anxious, or do you rehearse, reflect, and ruminate on things that lead to bitterness? Practice writing a three- or four-sentence gospel sermon to your anxious heart below.

This past week, you completed the Session Three personal study in your books. If you weren't able to do so, no big deal! You can still follow along with the questions, be involved in the discussion, and watch the video. When you are ready to begin, open up your time in prayer and push play on Video Three for Session Three.

WATCH

Write down any thoughts, verses, or things you want to remember as you watch the video for Session Three of Anxious.

REVIEW SESSION THREE PERSONAL STUDY

From Day One: What did God tell Jonah to do, and what was his response? How did God respond to Jonah's disobedience?

From Day Two: What fears do you have that keep you from obedience when you encounter a command in God's Word or direction from the Holy Spirit?

From Day Three: How did the people of Nineveh respond to Jonah's message, and what did God do?

From Day Four: What does the end of the Book of Jonah tell you about God (Jonah 4:10-11)?

From Day Five: Other than the birds and the flowers, what else can we consider that Jesus cares for and sustains?

FROM THIS WEEK'S STUDY

As a group, review this week's memory verse.

But seek first the kingdom of God and his righteousness, and all these things will be provided for you. Therefore don't worry about tomorrow, because tomorrow will worry about itself. Each day has enough trouble of its own.

MATTHEW 6:33-34

DISCUSS

In this session, we looked at the Book of Jonah and studied the story of God mercifully and creatively offering Jonah a second chance. If you're comfortable with it, share about a time God gave you a second chance.

This session's main idea is "Jesus is our King in the fight against anxiety." What are some things you've made "King" in your life that contribute to anxiety? Why is Jesus a better King than those things?

What verses from this session have stuck with you and helped you as you fight to make Jesus King of your life and battle against your fears?

This week's memory verse is about seeking the kingdom. Try to recite the verse together as a group. Then, talk about what God might have you pursue individually or as a group for His kingdom this week.

PRAY

Take turns sharing prayer requests and thanking God for the power of His forgiveness and the power He gives us to forgive others. Spend the remainder of your time in prayer. Maybe, if you sit in a circle, each woman can pray for the woman on her right—that she will be able to seek first God's kingdom and find freedom from her worries.

To access the teaching sessions, use the instructions in the back of your Bible study book.

ANXIOUS MOSES

JESUS IS OUR STRENGTH IN THE FIGHT AGAINST ANXIETY

BUT MOSES SAID TO THE PEOPLE, **"DON'T BE AFRAID.** STAND FIRM AND SEE THE LORD'S SALVATION THAT HE WILL ACCOMPLISH FOR YOU TODAY; FOR THE EGYPTIANS YOU SEE TODAY, YOU WILL NEVER SEE AGAIN. THE **LORD WILL FIGHT FOR YOU,** AND YOU MUST BE QUIET."

Exodus 14:13-14

DAY ONE
WHEN THE BABY BASKET ISN'T SO CUTE

Exodus 3; Isaiah 6:1-8 and 1 John 3:1

In school this week, my five-year-old daughter did a "Baby Moses Craft." She colored a little baby, glued it to a basket picture, and stuck the whole thing to a sponge. Then she was supposed to put the sponge in a bowl of water and watch it float like baby Moses. Yippee! It floated! Adorable! Fun!

Right?

Here's some other words I think of when I look at this sweet little craft:

- drowning;

- separation-anxiety;

- trauma;

- genocide;

- slavery;

- general horribleness.

I have to confess something. I don't love crafts. But my daughter did love the craft. It's just that I felt less "Yippee!" and more disconcerted by the image. When you're little and cutting a piece of sponge to put a baby picture on, it's harder to imagine the gravity of that historical account than when you're a mother with babies of your own.

Here's the thing. The reality of that little sponge craft represents a real time when baby boys were being taken from their mothers' arms and slaughtered.

The sponge craft rested on a rough situation.

When we were in the process of adopting our daughter, Joy, we watched hours of video training and read required books detailing the trauma a child goes through when he/she is separated from his/her birth mother. We were told again and again that every international adoption is a "special needs adoption." We learned about how, when a mother instinctively rocks her baby, his/her inner ear is stimulated, which allows him/her to learn and helps his/her brain make connections. We learned about the mental and physical distress an infant goes through when he/she is unable to be with his/her mother.

I say all this to tell you Moses' experience with anxiety probably didn't start when he saw an on-fire bush not burning. It probably didn't even start when he killed an Egyptian and ran. It more likely started when he was a baby, separated from his mother and put into a basket into a river—by himself.

All adoptions are special needs adoptions birthed out of trauma. So here we are at the outset of Exodus 3. Up until this point, Moses had spent his life in a foreign family, discovered he was adopted, found out his people were mistreated slaves, and fled after killing an Egyptian. And now there's a bush on fire that's not burning up, and a voice is coming out of it.

Read Exodus 3. Draw a picture of what happened to Moses in this chapter.

Look at verse 1. What mundane and faithful thing was Moses doing when the angel of the LORD appeared to him in the burning bush?

It's often in the mundane moments of faithfulness that the Spirit will break through and prompt us, speak to us, move us, call us to action.

What are some parts of your life that feel mundane right now?

When the Lord called my family to adopt, I was active in a small group and walking in obedience in small, unseen, mundane ways. As I told you in the Session Three teaching video, the Spirit broke my heart over abandoned girls in China with special needs while I drove to the grocery store because I'd forgotten to pick up dishwasher detergent.

There's nothing like experiencing the supernatural, all-powerful God while you go about your natural, powerless-looking life—picking up detergent or taking care of sheep.

Reread verses 2–6.

How did Moses respond to God in verse 6?

What does Moses' response to God tell us about him and his feelings?

The way Moses responded, covering his face and feeling "afraid" (v. 6), as the Bible tells us, reminds me of when Isaiah entered the Lord's throne room in Isaiah 6 "and the train of his robe filled the temple" (v. 1b, ESV).

Real quick, flip to Isaiah 6 and read verses 1-5. How did Isaiah respond to what he saw?

He was terrified, "undone" (v. 5, NKJV), sharply aware of his unworthiness as he stood in the presence of the One who is Holy.

Read Isaiah 6:6-8. What led the undone Isaiah to go from "I am ruined" (v. 5a) to "Here I am. Send me" (v. 8b)?

God is merciful.

Looking back at Moses' story, here's something cool. Once God had his attention with the bush, He said Moses' name twice. Apparently, in ancient Jewish culture, saying someone's name twice was a way to show friendship, affection, and endearment.[1]

How beautiful that even as He revealed His impossible-to-comprehend power and commanded Moses to do a hard/scary/terrifying/life-threatening thing, He addressed Moses lovingly—as a friend, as beloved.

Do you ever read God's Word or hear about it in church and feel afraid, like Moses did, by what you encounter? Are there specific verses in the Bible that cause you to feel afraid?

The Bible isn't warm and fuzzy, and God isn't a teddy bear. I've often neglected the Lord because I was afraid of Him. I'd read the words of Jesus to His disciples, as He told them about the cost of following Him. Sometimes, Christian persecution overseas will break into my mind, and I long for comfort, fluff, and ignorance.

But that's because I forget how He speaks. Yes, He has the power to destroy all life with a flood or fire or just His voice. But that's not how He talks to His own. He calls me "daughter." He says, "Scarlet, Scarlet . . ."

Read 1 John 3:1. How should this reality affect our fear of God?

Because we're loved children, we can fear God with awe but approach Him as Dad. We can walk in obedience, knowing He doesn't promise us an easy life, but He promises us His love and presence and His strength as our own.

Read Exodus 3:7-11.

What did God ask Moses to do and how did Moses respond?

What does God's assignment for Moses tell us about His character and His purposes?

The compassion and care of the Lord is so evident in these verses. He told Moses that He heard the cries and saw the pain of His people and that He was going to rescue them. And He wanted to use Moses to do it. How crazy is that?

Read Exodus 3:12 and copy it down.

In the space below, I want you to write out the things you're afraid God could ask of you. Then write, "I will certainly be with you" after each one. God doesn't send us alone. When we go, we go in His care, His strength and His name. Whatever your worry, ask God to help you trust Him.

DAY TWO

WHY FEAR ACTUAL SCARY THINGS WHEN YOU COULD FEAR CONVERSATION?

Exodus 3:13-22 and John 8:56-58

I know, OK? I know we live in a world of legitimate problems. I know there are countless things a normal person should fear. There's no need for me to make a list of them because you know what they are. The grown-up realities. We can worry about evil, abuse, pain, and death. Those are the real scary things. So why is it that my number one anxiety often goes like this:

If I say this, and she says that, then what do I say? And if I do say that, will I say it the right way? What will she say? If she says something I don't think she'll say, then what should I say? What if I just don't say anything? But what if she's super upset because I don't say anything? What if Jesus could just come back right now and say something before I have to say something or not say something?

Maybe you're rolling your eyes because you would never be anxious about a situation so silly. But I'm sure you worry about other things that aren't exactly life or death.

Most of us do it. And I would argue that neglecting the actual scary things and instead worrying over relational awkwardness or other small concerns is a very human, very timeless way to respond to bigger problems. Most of the times I'm afraid of silly things like conversations that don't exist, I've got much more serious stresses in the back of my mind.

Spoiler alert—you're about to read about Moses doing exactly this.

Read Exodus 3:13. God told Moses to go lead the Israelites, who, mind you, had been slaves for four hundred years, out of Egypt. If God told you to do something of that magnitude, what would your first questions be?

God told Moses to return to a place where he was known as a murderer-runaway and rescue a nation of slaves. And if you read the conversation, it sounds a lot like, *If I say this . . . and they say this . . . what do I say next?*

Anxiety can lead us to focus on the wrong things. The little things.

Imagine you're standing in the middle of the road on a hill and a speeding car is coming right toward you. The normal-fear response would be to fear the imminent danger and respond by getting out of the way. The best response to that situation would be for your legs to start moving out of the path of the car. But what if you focused on smaller worries? *Hold on. What are you going to do if your insurance doesn't cover this hospital bill? If you dive out of the way and lose your phone, who will call the police? Please don't ruin your favorite jeans.*

When a car is about to hit you, you don't have time for anxiety. You get out of the way of the danger. You don't worry about insurance or cell phone placement.

Moses did the same things we do. He focused on problems when what he needed to do was remember God called him to this and God would carry him through this.

Do you find Moses' imperfect faith comforting? Why or why not?

We can take comfort knowing the heroes of the faith were shaky people like us. People who questioned God's plan. People who probably had anxiety rather than feeling awe and confidence in their interaction with the great "I AM."

Read Exodus 3:13-22.

In verses 13-14, Moses basically asked God His name, and God gave a seemingly strange answer. What did God say His name is?

What did He mean? Do a quick Google® search or look inside of a study Bible to see what you find about this name for God. Record your findings in the space below. (And share some with your group when you meet together!).

I AM tells us God exists. In fact, "I AM WHO I AM" means God must exist. God is the one and only Necessary Being. That leads us to the truth that nothing can exist without God giving it existence. I AM WHO I AM. God can't not exist. And everything else can't exist without Him. But perhaps the most significant application of this name God gave Moses is that God has, as John Piper put it, "drawn near to us in Jesus Christ."[2]

Read John 8:56-58. In verse 58, we see Jesus said something very powerful. What did He say, and what does it have to do with God's name in Exodus 13?

Jesus was claiming the name of the great "I am." Jesus was telling the world that He isn't just a teacher, or just a healer, or just a worker of miracles. He is I AM. He is God. He is existence itself in a human body, come to save the world.

That's who Moses had on his team and that's who we have forever. We don't have to be anxious because Jesus is I AM. I AM existed before anything else did and everything that is, *is*, because He is. He can handle your awkward conversation no matter how it goes down.

I AM came into this broken, sad, scary place to live and die and rise again. He is more powerful than even death.

When we look at Moses' life, we see a weak man used powerfully by a strong God. Isn't that a relief? God doesn't need us to "be awesome." He's awesome. He wants us to love Him and obey Him—even when we don't feel brave, even when we fumble over our words and prayers and responses to His leading in our lives.

In the space below, list a few of God's awesome attributes that are on display in this story and thank Him for being so good.

DAY THREE
A BROKEN THYROID AND
A GOD WHO SEES

Exodus 14:1-14

The year before writing this Bible study, I had a drawn-out season of HARD.

I began suffering mysterious symptoms that lasted for months. I was bounced around to different doctors and machines, ultimately leading to tumors at the end of whatever is the opposite of a rainbow. The doctors thought I had cancer, but they weren't sure. It was a rough run. I knew that because of my relationship with Christ, I could have (and should have) "count[ed] it all joy" when I experienced "trials of various kinds" (Jas. 1:2, ESV). But the thing is, I wasn't joyful. I wasn't thankful. Instead, I was sad and lonely. Scared and weak. I didn't understand why God was allowing my health to fail me. He was allowing a big heap of painful and scary and hard things, and I had more questions than answers.

What questions did you ask God in your last drawn-out season of HARD?

Read Exodus 14:1-4.

What did God tell Moses to do here?

What did God tell Moses Pharaoh would do?

The first handful of verses in Exodus 14 are striking. We've skipped ahead a little, but what's happened, in a nutshell, is God did as He said He would, and He used Moses to free the Hebrews from slavery. Moses then led them through the wilderness toward Canaan, "the promised land," where they would be free to flourish.

But then the story takes a turn. In chapter 14, we see that while God's people were probably still exhaling, trouble was coming again. Pharaoh changed his mind about freeing them and wanted to take them back as slaves. And, prepare yourself, it was GOD'S PLAN. What?!

Can you think of a time in your life when you felt God was causing or allowing something hard or negative to happen to you? What were the circumstances?

God, the Creator and Sovereign I AM, is so involved and in control of what's going on in the world that He hardened Pharaoh's heart and led him to pursue the Israelites with his army. And it wasn't because He's mean or wanted to scare anyone. He wanted, as He told Moses here, to "receive glory" (v. 4). His plan was to break through time and space, as He has done so many times and still does and still will do, to remind humanity that He is BIG and sea-splittingly trustworthy.

Now let's look at verses 5–12.

What happened to the Israelites in these verses?

How did the Israelites respond? (See verses 10-12.)

How do you think you would have responded in this situation?

If you've taken a good look at the darkness inside your own heart, you'll nod in understanding to the response of God's people.

How many times have you seen this play out in the movies, in the lives of your friends, in your own family? It's human nature to want to return to familiar problems rather than face an unknown danger. We often return to what we know, even when we understand it's bad for us.

What do you think was at the root of the Israelites' response to the danger they faced?

In his book, *The Knowledge of the Holy*, A. W. Tozer wrote, "What comes into our minds when we think about God is the most important thing about us."[3]

What comes into your mind when you think about God?

I look at this story and wonder what I'd be thinking and feeling if I were an Israelite. Depending on how well I'm understanding or trusting God at the time, I might have felt shocked or angry with God. I may have doubted His goodness and provision. I may have, like the Israelites, blamed the guy/girl/institution leading me.

Look at Moses' response to the people in verses 13 and 14 and copy it in the space below.

When I had my thyroid taken out last year, I went into that surgery expecting to wake up to a cancer diagnosis and a mortality rate. But God healed me. There was no cancer, and once my broken thyroid was out, He restored my health and most of my energy.

God is able on the days full of joy. God is able even when you get the hard diagnosis. God is able no matter what circumstance you find yourself in. "Stand firm and see the LORD's salvation" (Ex. 14:13). The God who allows cancer can kill cancer. The God who allows pharaohs to chase can drown them in the sea. But we'll get to that tomorrow.

As you go about the rest of your day, meditate on Moses' response to the people at the end of today's passage. "Don't be afraid. Stand firm and see the LORD's salvation that he will accomplish for you today . . . The LORD will fight for you, and you must be quiet" (Ex. 14:13-14).

DAY FOUR
BUT WHAT IF MY DAUGHTER DIES?

Exodus 14:15-31 and Matthew 6:34

I went through a season of major anxiety when my oldest daughter was about three. I became obsessed with the thought that I could lose her. I was constantly aware that she could die.

There were days it was all I could think about. I had bouts of hyperventilating and said no to anything fun if it sounded remotely dangerous. It was not a good phase.

How has your family had to deal with your anxiety in the past? How have your worries impacted them, and how have they responded?

Charles Spurgeon once said, "The worst evils of life are those which do not exist except in our imagination. If we had no troubles but real troubles, we should not have a tenth part of our present sorrows. We feel a thousand deaths in fearing one."[4]

In Matthew 6:34 (remember this verse from last week?), what did Jesus say NOT to worry about? Why?

Now read Exodus 14:15-18. In verses 17-18, God was explicit about why He was doing what He was doing. What is the reason He gave?

Sometimes, I experience suffering, and I can see glimmers of good in the midst of the bad. I see, as it's happening, some of the why God allows it. But other times, I don't see anything. There are situations in our lives that seem only evil and painful and hopeless. But this is exactly why we know not to look only at our own lives.

What you are doing right now, getting to know the character and greatness of God in His Word, is preparing you to trust God when you think you only see hopelessness. God's Word helps you fight with truth when you only feel fear. The Bible teaches you to recognize glory when, otherwise, you might only see pain.

Write down just three reasons God is worthy of glory at all times.

1.

2.

3.

All over the Old Testament, we see God in the stories of these heroes of the faith, like Moses, and we learn the way God acts and thinks.

All over the New Testament, we see Jesus sharing and showing His power. We learn that Jesus is the way to hope. That He brings redemption. He makes all things new. God's glory is displayed all over the place, and the more we see it the more we understand that as God is getting glory, He is bringing about our good.

Read Exodus 14:19-31.

Try to draw a picture of the miraculous things that happened.

What is your favorite part of this miracle? Why?

Read verse 31 again. How did God's people respond to what God did?

God parted the sea and led His people to safety. The result was that instead of fearing the unknowns and potentials for pain, they feared the Lord.

Anxiety crushes us because it makes us fear the wrong things.

What are some of the wrong things you're fearing right now?

When we fear the Lord, when we recognize He is worthy of our fear, awe, and glory, the smaller things that make us "feel a thousand deaths" are swallowed in the sea.[5]

When I focus on the glory of God, I don't find myself praying in a panic that my daughters won't die. I find myself praying for their souls, for their understanding of God's love, for their future callings to make Him known to their generation.

God is doing miracles all the time. And He uses regular, flawed, cowards like us. When we look to Him, see His power, and trust His plan, we find freedom from our fears.

Make a list in the space below. What would you like to see God do this week? Think of the people in your life who don't know Him—who don't know freedom and peace. Commit to praying for them this week and see what God will do. Ask the Lord to help you fear Him rather than the unknowns in your life.

DAY FIVE
IS THAT A FIRM NO?

Exodus 4:10-13 and Hebrews 3:1-3

I have this thing with my husband. I know husband-wifery is a team thing, but the problem is, I really like things to go my way.

Sometimes I want one thing, and he wants something else. I don't really want to be the boss. I don't want to do anything that will bankrupt us or ruin our kids. I just want everything I want to always happen immediately. Is that so much to ask? ☺

There are times, if you can believe it, I have a clearly amazing idea he should definitely be on board with, and he says, NO.

But then I ask, "Is that a firm no?"

I question his answer, in hopes it might change. (It works a lot by the way.)

Read Exodus 4:10.

In Exodus 4:10, Moses questioned God in hopes the plan might change.

What was Moses' excuse for not wanting to do what God told him to?

Look at verses 11-12. How did God respond?

Moses was persistent in his resistance. How did he respond to God in verse 13?

The story of Moses is a beautiful picture of God's faithfulness in the midst of our fear and hesitation. Moses was a worrying, doubting, God-questioning, messed up human, just like me and just like you, who did a really hard thing. And God was with him, just as He promised He would be.

Have you ever gotten to witness this in someone's life? When have you seen God use someone unlikely to do something impressively compassionate or miraculous?

Looking at and attempting to mimic Moses' obedience (no matter how fear-filled or questioning) is a wonderful idea. But the clearer, better way to move toward peace and obedience is by looking at and chasing after Someone else.

The story God was inviting Moses into wasn't actually about Moses. It was always about God.

Read Hebrews 3:1-3. Who is considered "worthy of more glory than Moses" (v. 3)?

In verse 3, the writer of Hebrews compared Jesus' superiority to Moses to a builder getting more honor than the house. What do you think this comparison tells us about God?

A created thing can't be better than the Creator. Jesus is the I AM, remember? Jesus is the builder of all things. Jesus created Moses and the stuttering, questioning, staff-raising miracles that came through him. Jesus is immeasurably greater than Moses.

What are some ways Jesus is better than Moses?

Moses confronted Pharaoh. Jesus confronted Satan, sin, and death.

Moses led from physical slavery to the promised land. Jesus leads from spiritual slavery to freedom.

Moses lifted up his staff to make a way for his people to cross the sea. Jesus lifted up His body to make a way for His people to cross from death to life.

Moses served, died, and was buried. Jesus served, died, was buried, left the grave behind, ascended to glory, lives forever, and rules the world every minute of every day.

So, yes, Moses was good, but Jesus is better.

Jesus is the reason anxious Moses could move forward and find freedom. Jesus is the reason anxious you can move forward into whatever God has planned. You are scared, but guess what? Jesus isn't.

What are some ways Jesus is better than you?

How do you need Jesus to be strong in you today?

As you go about the rest of your week, remember that you don't have to fight your way to peace. Jesus is your strength in the fight against anxiety. He will lead you through the waters, to the other side, to the promised land. And in the ways that matter most, He already has. He has saved you. In Jesus, you're on the other side of the sea, and it's time to rest.

This past week, you completed the Session Four personal study in your books. If you weren't able to do so, no big deal! You can still follow along with the questions, be involved in the discussion, and watch the video. When you are ready to begin, open up your time in prayer and push play on Video Four for Session Four.

WATCH

Write down any thoughts, verses, or things you want to remember as you watch the video for Session Four of Anxious.

REVIEW SESSION FOUR PERSONAL STUDY

From Day One: Do you ever read God's Word or hear about it in church and feel afraid, like Moses did, by what you encounter? Are there specific verses in the Bible that cause you to feel afraid?

From Day Two: In Exodus 3:14, God told Moses His name was I AM. What did you learn about this name as you studied it this week?

From Day Three: Can you think of a time in your life when you felt God was causing or allowing something hard or negative to happen to you? What were the circumstances?

From Day Four: In Matthew 6:34, what did Jesus say NOT to worry about? Why?

From Day Five: Compare and contrast Jesus with Moses. What can we learn from Moses, and why is Jesus better than Moses?

FROM THIS WEEK'S STUDY

As a group, review this week's memory verse.

But Moses said to the people, "Don't be afraid. Stand firm and see the LORD's salvation that he will accomplish for you today; for the Egyptians you see today, you will never see again. The LORD will fight for you, and you must be quiet."

EXODUS 14:13-14

DISCUSS

This week, we studied Moses. We saw him scared and sinful, but also obedient and faithful. He was fully a human and fully loved by God. He went through scary things, and He followed God to what looked like scary places in order to be used in accomplishing God's purpose for His people. If you're comfortable with it, tell your group about a time God asked you to do something hard or scary.

This session's main idea is "Jesus is our strength in the fight against anxiety." What are some things you lean on as "strength" that can't hold up under the weight of life? How is Jesus better?

What verses from this session have stuck with you from and helped you as you fight to make Jesus your strength as you battle against your fears?

PRAY

Take turns sharing prayer requests and thanking God for His strength that lets us rest. Thank Him for showing us how to walk with Him and for being merciful when we forget that it's His strength we depend on. Spend the remainder of your time in prayer. Pray specifically that you, as a group, would rely on the strength of the Spirit as you seek to love the people you've been scared to love and do the things you've been scared to do. Ask the Lord to unite your group and remove all anxiety that is keeping you from service to Him and peace in His Spirit.

To access the teaching sessions, use the instructions in the back of your Bible study book.

ANXIOUS ESTHER

JESUS IS SOVEREIGN IN OUR FIGHT AGAINST ANXIETY

IF YOU KEEP SILENT AT

THIS TIME, RELIEF AND

DELIVERANCE WILL COME

TO THE JEWISH PEOPLE

FROM ANOTHER PLACE,

BUT YOU AND YOUR

FATHER'S FAMILY WILL BE

DESTROYED. WHO KNOWS,

PERHAPS YOU HAVE COME

TO YOUR ROYAL POSITION

FOR SUCH A TIME AS THIS.

Esther 4:14

DAY ONE
A HAND-ME-DOWN BARBIE DREAM HOUSE AND A VERY ROMANTIC LOVE STORY

Esther 1-2 and Colossians 1:16-17

When I was in fifth grade, a neighbor from down the road gave me a hand-me-down Barbie® DreamHouse™. Pretty much all I remember from that year is locking myself in my room and playing out what I thought was the ULTIMATE romantic situation, over and over again.

I know this is what you're here for, so let me explain.

Barbie and Ken™ are at a party. Sorry, I meant to say a ball. They're at a ball. They're talking, laughing, waving goodbye to people. They both happen to be walking backward when they bump into each other and fall on the floor. Both clearly annoyed, they argue, in unison. "How dare you! Where do you thi—" And then, they pause. This is the moment that they both realize their whole lives have been leading up to this moment. And that they're destined for love.

That's the magic of playing dolls. Two lives (plastic dolls), led by the hands of destiny (tweenage Scarlet) to find each other, fall for each other, and "enjoy" a lengthy, awkward plastic doll kiss.

Would you believe this is a way I've taught my daughters about sovereignty? They have their own hand-me-down Barbie house (thanks Autumn) and their own plans for romantic doll destiny, and I want them to trust the powerful guidance of a loving God.

Now, God is not a preteen, and we're not brainless plastic dolls, but we can take comfort in the fact that He exists outside of our world, outside of time itself, and is in total control of every situation we experience. We are anxious Kens and worrying Barbies. But God is sovereign all the time.

As we study Esther this week, we're going to look at the sovereignty of God that exists even when life looks impossibly bad or scary, and we'll remember why and how that can nudge us toward peace.

Look up the word sovereignty in a dictionary, and write down the definitions you find in the space below.

As much as I'd like to be sovereign over my home and my life the way I was sovereign over my Barbies, I'm just not. To be sovereign is to possess supreme or ultimate power. I don't have power over the behavior of the people in my life, over the cells in their bodies doing what they're supposed to do, over their safety, or even their happiness.

When God allows pain I don't understand, probably nothing is more comforting to me than to remember He has ultimate power over all things.

Let's look at this idea through some of the scarier situations that went down in the life of a woman named Esther.

Read Esther 1–2 and try to see if you can find any mentions of God. Did you find any?

Esther is the only book in the Bible that doesn't mention God one single time. How strange is that? How is there a book in the Bible, authored by God, all about God, that fails to mention God? In reading commentaries on this book, I learned that not only is God not mentioned, but neither are there any recorded prayers or references to the Torah (the first five books of the Hebrew Bible) or the temple.[1]

So why is this book here? As we'll see, it's all about sovereignty.

Esther was a Jew living in Persia being raised by her cousin, Mordecai. During those days, the Jews were in exile. They were religious minorities in a God-opposing culture led by an absolute monarch.

So in the first chapter of Esther, we learn that King Ahasuerus (you've probably also heard him called by his Greek name, Xerxes) was getting rid of his queen, Vashti, and looking for a new one. That's the kind of thing he could just do without any consequences.

Look back at Esther 1:10–12.

Why was the king mad at Queen Vashti?

What did the king's advisers encourage him to do? (See verses 13–21.)

Esther 2:10 says Esther didn't reveal her ethnicity because Mordecai told her not to. Have you ever experienced anxiety over being different than people around you, whether it was because of physical, socioeconomic, ethnic, or racial differences? If yes, what happened?

Have you ever experienced anxiety because of someone in power who was doing things you disagreed with? Explain.

How do you tend to cope with this sort of anxiety?

King Ahasuerus had absolute earthly power. That's scary. When there are employers or presidents or family members whom we don't agree with in any position of power, it can lead us to feel insecure, especially when politics or racism are involved, like what we see in Esther's story.

When we see people in power who are making sinful decisions, it's tempting to believe God's gone missing.

Read Colossians 1:16-17. Write the following in your own words, "He is before all things, and by him all things hold together" (v. 17).

The story of Esther, the story of Colossians, and the story of the universe itself is that God never goes missing. Whether you're struggling with a circumstance, a relationship, or a person, you can fight your anxiety by holding on to the truth, the reality, that God is before all things. He is powerful over all powerful people. He doesn't need to be named, but He can't be ignored because He holds life itself together. When life looks like bad decisions and chaos and a big mess we can't control, we don't have to control. The sovereign God is leading the way.

In the space below, list the situations in your life that look bad. Surrender them to the Lord and trust He will hold you together. He will hold everything together. You can trust He will sustain His people just like He sustained the Israelites through Esther and Mordecai.

DAY TWO
A SNIFFLE, A SURGERY, AND A GIANT TOOTH

Esther 3:1-11; Psalm 4:8; Psalm 121:2-4; Romans 8:28 and 1 Peter 1:8

Recently, my daughter, Joy, had her last of three ear surgeries. I'd been up all night with another sick kid the night before and woke up to an alarm at 4 a.m. to take Joy to the hospital. My husband couldn't take her because he was also sick. That was already a less-than-ideal day, but while I was sitting in the waiting room, I felt a telltale sign of a dental abscess (not my first abscess rodeo—I've got troubled teeth). I called my dentist friend, drove to the dentist chair, and had to have my largest molar pulled out of my head for an hour and a half.

A few things:

1. Why does it take an hour and a half?

2. Always say yes to laughing gas. Always.

3. Expressions like "When it rains, it pours" exist for a reason.

4. The week of sickness, surgery, and emergency molar removal has filled me with more gratitude than I've had in a long time.

Isn't that weird?

We looked at this James verse earlier, but let's look again—James 1:2 says, "Consider it a great joy, my brothers and sisters, whenever you experience various trials."

I used to read that and feel panicked by it. I thought various trials were always coming for me—that failure, danger, and pillagement were around every corner and that if I didn't do every Christian thing just right, I'd miss the joy, ruin the moment, and experience all the things I was afraid of for no good purpose at all. I was missing the whole point.

Every living and active word of the Bible points us not just to the steps to take in trials, but to a sovereign Savior, whose perfection is completely given to us and whose power is always working.

Today, we follow more of Esther's story as she took steps in a terrifying trial as a great God worked behind the scenes.

Read Esther 3:1-11.

What do we see Haman attempted to do?

At this point, did it look like he would succeed in his objective?

Have you ever had one of those moments when it just felt like your whole life was falling apart? What is the hardest season you can remember in your life?

What did you do?

What did God do?

Look up 1 Peter 1:3-9. Focus on verse 8 and copy it in the space below.

We can see our problems, and they scare us. We don't physically get to see God right now, but we love Him. We believe in Him. We can rejoice, knowing He is at work even throughout abscess emergencies, political emergencies, and personal trauma we didn't see coming.

Turn to Romans 8:28.

What does God do in every situation for those who love Him?

What are some trials you're walking through right now that you can praise God for today, knowing He is at work and will use it for good?

God is sovereign, which means He's never not working.

Read Psalm 121:2-4.

Where does our help come from?

What is God called in verses 3 and 4?

What does verse 4 tell us God does not do?

When I was little, I couldn't fall asleep unless I heard my parents watching TV and puttering around. I didn't want to be awake when they were asleep because then I'd feel alone and scared. I sensed safety when I knew they were awake and could take care of me. I trusted them to protect me if something happened while I was off the clock. So I've always loved this truth—that my Protector, the only one who actually has real control over my safety, never sleeps.

Read and copy Psalm 4:8 in the space below.

Life with Jesus means hope for later and abundant life today. It means trials are temporary, and joy is eternal because we place our hope in His hands that run the world and never tire.

You might be having a less-than-ideal day, or week, or moment in your home, but you have a "let us not grow weary" hope in your heart (Gal. 6:9, ESV). You can have peace instead of panic because you have access to the God who is in control, even when it feels like your Hamans are going to win.

Write a prayer asking the Lord to help you trust He is working in situations that look hopeless. Ask that He will help you rest and trust and sleep, knowing He is awake, present, and loving.

DAY THREE
A SWAT REFLEX AND A BUNK BED RESCUE

Esther 4 and Romans 11:36

My most "for such a time as this" memory involves my SWAT officer dad. When I was twelve, my little sister was exploring the bedroom of a little girl named Beth. I was loitering around with the grown-ups waiting for dinner to be ready when our hosts asked if we wanted a tour of the house.

They took us from room to room and then we got to Beth's. Beth was four with a little blonde bob and a bunk bed. For whatever reason, right as we walked in, everything seemed to change to slow-motion as we watched little Beth dive headfirst from the top bunk toward the floor.

My adoptive dad and his SWAT muscles were, thankfully, in the room at that moment, and he calmly raised his hands and caught Beth by the ankles right before her head hit the ground.

It was a little bit like witnessing a miracle. The strong, trained officer was standing at the right place at the right time to save a little girl from breaking her neck. That's the type of providence we see in the life of Esther.

Read Esther 4. In verse 7, what did Mordecai share that he learned was to happen to the Jews?

In chapter 4, the messenger relayed information between Mordecai and Esther, ending on Mordecai's famous plea, "Who knows, perhaps you have come to your royal position for such a time as this" (v. 14b).

Mordecai suggested Esther's position and her opportunity to serve her people wasn't simply a coincidence. Mordecai, a believer, knew God orchestrated everything, and maybe He put Esther in this position of power so that she could save God's people.

Look up Romans 11:36 (CSB translation) and fill in the blanks.

For from _____ and through _____ and to _____ are all things. To _____ be the glory forever. Amen.

Guys, please never forget that God has all the power. He doesn't have some of the power. He doesn't have most of the power. From Him and through Him and to Him are all things.

Sometimes that means Paul Wessel is standing at the right bunk bed at the right time. Sometimes that means Esther is in the right court in front of the right king to save a people from genocide.

Read Esther 4:15-17. What brave action did Esther plan to take?

Courage like that looks impossible from the outside. We think only "super Christians" do super brave things. But the longer I live, the more I see that God takes anxious people with simple obedience to accomplish extraordinary things in His sovereignty.

How do you think Esther may have felt in the days of fasting and planning to go before the king?

The Bible doesn't tell us how she felt, but I bet she felt great anxiety. She couldn't know how it would go. She didn't know if she'd be killed or banished (like Vashti) or if lives would be saved. But she trusted in God's sovereignty.

Why is it comforting to read about Esther and all the uncertainty she walked through that led to freedom for her people?

Maybe you haven't recently witnessed a miraculous moment. Maybe life feels ho-hum, and God just feels far away, and maybe that makes you nervous. Take heart. God uses every season and every circumstance to draw us closer to Himself. (See Romans 8.) When life looks scary and faith feels hard, remember that God is sovereign as you fight to feel peace.

Try to list three situations you've witnessed or been through where you saw the sovereignty of God on display.

1.

2.

3.

Close out your study time today thanking Him for His power and care and asking Him to help you do what He's called you to today, trusting that He is working, He is present, and He loves you.

DAY FOUR
DID GOD REALLY FIND YOUR PHONE?

Esther 5 and Esther 7:1–6

When my oldest was six, she gave me the following pep talk:

Mommy, God knew this was going to happen. From the moment Adam and Eve sinned, He knew you were going to lose your phone.

I thought it was hilarious and adorable and such a churched-kid thing to say. Obviously, I'd lost my phone. But I didn't think to involve God in the issue.

Like, "Hey God, I know You are probably busy caring for orphans and widows and listening to prayers about peoples' cancer and stuff, but can You just help me find my phone because I haven't checked Instagram in a few seconds?"

I often live parts of life as if God's not involved. Sure, He's involved in big things. But, like, lost iPhones? It just seems like a job not for Him. In our fight against anxiety, we need to know everything is a job for Him.

Today, we'll continue to look at God's involvement in the details of Esther's story.

Read Esther 5.

What did Esther ask the king?

How did the king respond to Esther's request?

Once again, we witness a "coincidence" of good fortune for Esther.

I used to kind of giggle when older Christians would talk about how God answered their prayers about finding their missing car keys or keeping them safe on airplanes. I failed to recognize what those older saints knew to be true—God is in the details, the little ones and the big ones. Recognizing He is present and active in every circumstance is an excellent way to quiet anxiety.

Throughout the rest of the Book of Esther, we read about a banquet with the king and Haman. We see Esther requested another banquet and then a drunk Haman left and saw Mordecai. I'll say the horrifying part as unobtrusively as I can. Haman got mad and ordered that Mordecai be impaled on a big stake on top of having already ordered that all Jews be killed in chapter 3.[2] We good?

Read Esther 7:1-6. What was the first thing the king said to Esther in this chapter, and how did she respond?

The gist of it is, the night before, the king had trouble sleeping. (See Esth. 6:1.) While the royal chronicles were being read to him, he heard about how Mordecai saved his life. So in the morning when Haman was about to tell the king he wanted Mordecai dead, the king ordered the opposite. He made Haman honor Mordecai. You can read the rest of the story in Esther 8-10. Long story short, Esther and Mordecai worked with the king to save the Jews. There were celebration banquets; Mordecai became second in command; the Jews prospered. That's the story.

There's no amen. There's no prayer. There's no tell-all theological explanation in the Book of Esther. But let's read between the lines.

Let's move ahead to the New Testament. Look up the following verses and write what it says about God next to the reference. *Some of these verses may look familiar because we studied them earlier this week!*

Romans 8:28

_____

Ephesians 1:11

_____

Colossians 1:16-17

_____

1 Timothy 6:15-16

_____

Which of these verses is most encouraging to you and why?

What would you do differently this week if you totally believed these verses were true?

No king, no ruler, no evil of any kind can keep God from caring for His people. Remember this as you wait for your biopsy results. Remember this when you get frustrated with your colicky newborn. Remember this when you get ready to share Jesus with your neighbor. Remember God is there, and He is sovereign over every small, massive, and medium thing in your life.

I want to challenge you today to include God in the little things. Bring your small concerns and your big ones and trust He is working behind the scenes in ways you can't see. He is looking on you with favor as the king looked on Esther. The difference is you don't have to worry or wonder about it. You don't have to hope your King doesn't change. Your King is perfect and powerful and favors you forever in Jesus.

List some of the little things that are on your mind today.

Now list the big ones.

What do you hope to see God do in each circumstance you wrote down?

In the space below, pray about some of these little and big things and ask God to speak to you in the details. Ask Him for an awareness of His presence and His providence in your life and a faith that says "I trust You" when you can't understand what He's doing.

DAY FIVE
THE PSALM I LEARNED IN HIGH SCHOOL

Psalm 103 and Hebrews 11:1,6

In tenth grade, my teacher made us memorize Psalm 103. I'm thirty-four, and I could still say it in my sleep.

Bless the LORD, O my soul,
and all that is within me,
bless his holy name!
Bless the LORD, O my soul,
and forget not all his benefits (vv. 1-2, ESV).

Read Psalm 103.

Look closely at verses 3-13. List what "his benefits" are below.

In the following blanks, personalize these verses a bit and list what God has done for you in each of these ways.

A sin of mine He forgave

A way He healed me

A time He showed me mercy

A way He renewed me

Which of those benefits is most meaningful to you right now, in this season of your life? Why?

The Book of Esther may not mention God, but we see so many of His behind-the-scenes benefits. We see Him redeem His people from the pit. We see Him execute acts of righteousness and give justice to the oppressed. We see His compassion and grace toward sinful people.

Read Psalm 103:19 and copy it below.

If I had to summarize the Book of Esther, I would do it by quoting Psalm 103:19. The Lord rules over all. That's it.

Paul Tripp spoke about the Book of Esther like this:

This God who seems absent is actually working to protect and preserve His story. You shouldn't conclude, because you can't see the hand of God, that God isn't at work anymore [than] you should conclude that the sun isn't shining because you're in your basement and you can't see it. These are these moments where you have to do what Hebrews 11 says, "You must believe that God exists and He rewards those who seek Him." I'm not going to give way to belief in the functional death of my Redeemer even in moments where I do not see His hand.[3]

Do you ever feel like God is absent in your life? On the scale below, mark down how tangibly you're currently experiencing His presence.

| 1 | 2 | 3 | 4 | 5 | 6 | 7 | 8 | 9 | 10 |

I don't feel God near.   God feels close to me.

It's so difficult to walk through seasons of life when God feels absent. If you're a believer, you know He's there. But sometimes you sense Him, and other times, He feels far away.

What are some ways you can pursue communication with God when He feels far away?

Turn to Hebrews 11:6. What do we need to please God?

What *is* faith? (Look at Heb. 11:1 for the biblical definition.)

When I read the Book of Esther, I see proof after proof after proof that God is working. Look at your own life. Maybe it's been some time since your relationship with God felt ablaze, but look at His blessings in your life. Your life is hard, but has He provided? Your life is sometimes scary, but has He protected?

List some of the ways God met your needs during those harder seasons when He felt far off.

You can believe in a God you can't see. You can trust He's working in your life even if your life looks like a bunch of Hamans and unfair beauty contests and conversations that could ruin you.

Esther went through a lot, and she came through it prosperous—not because she was awesome, but because God is. He had a plan for her, for her cousin, and for His beloved people. And He has a plan for you too. You don't have to save the day. God has already saved it. He's saved you. He's so, so powerful and nothing can touch Him. "The Lord rules over all." You can rest.

Pray through your anxiety by praising God for the work He does that you cannot see. Thank Him for being faithful and above all things.

This past week, you completed the Session Five personal study in your books. If you weren't able to do so, no big deal! You can still follow along with the questions, be involved in the discussion, and watch the video. When you are ready to begin, open up your time in prayer and push play on Video Five for Session Five.

WATCH

Write down any thoughts, verses, or things you want to remember as you watch the video for Session Five of *Anxious.*

FROM THIS WEEK'S STUDY

As a group, review this week's memory verse.

If you keep silent at this time, relief and deliverance will come to the Jewish people from another place, but you and your father's family will be destroyed. Who knows, perhaps you have come to your royal position for such a time as this.

ESTHER 4:14

REVIEW SESSION FIVE PERSONAL STUDY

From Day One: Esther 2:10 says Esther didn't reveal her ethnicity because Mordecai told her not to. Have you ever experienced anxiety over being different than people around you, whether it was because of physical, socioeconomic, ethnic, or racial differences? If yes, what happened?

From Day Two: Have you ever had one of those moments where it just felt like your whole life was falling apart? What is the hardest season you can remember in your life?

From Day Three: Why is it comforting to read about Esther and all the uncertainty she walked through that led to freedom for her people?

From Day Four: How do you approach God with the little things? Did you see God in the smaller details of your life this week?

From Day Five: Which of God's benefits, as laid out in Psalm 103, is most meaningful to you right now, in this season of your life? Why?

DISCUSS

This week we studied Esther. We looked at a book of the Bible where God is harder to find. We read between the lines, and we learned that though life is scary and complicated and people are sinful and messed up, God is always working things together for the good of those who love Him.

Did you learn anything new about the story of Esther this week? Share with your group.

What are you going through right now that causes anxiety because you can't see God's purpose in it? What do you think God's purpose might be? Share with your group and ask them to lift you up in prayer.

Which Bible verse was most impactful to you this week? Why?

This session's main idea is "Jesus is sovereign in our fight against anxiety." What are some action steps you can take this week to help yourself remember God is in control and He is trustworthy?

PRAY

Take turns sharing prayer requests and thanking God for being above all things and taking care of us. Pray He might use you to help people find spiritual freedom the way He used Esther to redeem the Jews. Ask Him to give you compassion for others and to dwell on His goodness and power rather than on the brokenness you see in the world.

To access the teaching sessions, use the instructions in the back of your Bible study book.

ANXIOUS PRAYER

PRAYER IS OUR POSTURE IN
THE FIGHT AGAINST ANXIETY

HUMBLE YOURSELVES, THEREFORE, UNDER THE MIGHTY HAND OF GOD, SO THAT HE MAY EXALT YOU AT THE PROPER TIME, **CASTING ALL YOUR CARES** ON HIM, BECAUSE HE CARES ABOUT YOU.

1 Peter 5:6–7

DAY ONE
JESUS TOOK MY BIRD AND SAW AWAY

1 Peter 5:6-7

I have a bunch of snapshot memories of the year my parents were getting divorced. I was very young, but I know there was a barbeque. A trampoline. A secret rock in the yard with nooks where I would stash pennies. I remember being in a lawyer's office with a copy machine and colored Wite-Out®. There are images of Grandma Marlene coming to stay with us to take care of me for way longer than usual.

I didn't understand my family was splitting apart. I didn't know whether to be sad or scared yet.

Grandma Marlene was amazing. She'd sit me on her lap outside by the pretty yellow flowers and sing hymns. So many hymns.

I'm so happy and here's the reason why;
Jesus took my burdens all awayyy.
Now, I'm singin' aaaas the days go byyyyy;
Jesus took my burdens all away.[1]

I loved the songs. But that one confused me.

"Jesus took my burdens all away" sounded to me a whole lot like, "Jesus took my bird and saw away."

I didn't understand why Jesus wanted a bird and saw and why my Grandma was so happy He took hers.

I got older and figured out the lyric misunderstanding but remained confused about how, specifically, to give Jesus my burdens. I'd sit through church youth events as a teenager and hear adults plead, "Come forward and leave your burdens at the cross!"

And I'd obey and think as hard as I could, *BURDENS, HERE, I LEAVE YOU. AT THIS CROSS MURAL IN THIS HIGH SCHOOL GYMNASIUM. ABRA CADABRA! AND AMEN!*

I so wanted my burdens to go away. I so wanted God to help me. But goodness—I didn't know how to do my part. Maybe you've wondered about that too. We all have burdens. What can we do with them?

Write 1 Peter 5:6-7 in the space below and circle the first two words.

When I first saw that and realized that it came before the "cast your anxiety" command, I felt like I'd cracked a secret code! So THAT'S how you do it! That's how you cast your cares on God! You humble yourself!

Wait—oh no—another abstract-sounding command.

Look up the word *humility* in the dictionary and write down what you find.

In the original Greek, *humility* denotes "not rising far from the ground"[2] and *humble yourself* means "to make low, bring low."[3]

The season I read that, I actually started praying on my knees. I'd always had a bit of an aversion to on-my-knees praying because once I discovered God loved me, not because of what I do, but because of what Jesus did, I relished in my freedom to pray with my eyes open, to pray in the middle of a meal or the end instead of the beginning. *Freeeeedooooom!*

But when I read that, I wanted to physically lower my body when I was talking to God. To train my body to remind my brain that I am low, that I am aware of God's bigness and power and my own weakness and frailty.

It was an incredible season where I tasted supernatural peace more often than I ever had before.

Write some other practical ways you can think of to "humble yourself" before God.

Here's the incredible thing. When I humbled myself, when I came before the Lord, lowly in Spirit, "casting my cares" on Him was a natural response. It just sort of happened. I remembered my status, as a created being, wholly dependent on a good, perfect, loving Father, and all those worries seemed to float to Him because I remembered He knows what to do. After I humbled myself, I was able to hum to "Jesus took my bird and saw away." (I don't think I did, but I could have!) After I humbled myself, I could smile, because I actually meant it, because I actually felt it.

I know this may not look exactly the same for each of us in our individual lives on our individual days, but God has promised to provide grace for each one of us as we humble ourselves before Him and cast our cares on Him.

Use this space to draw a picture of a time in your life when you felt free from burdens. How old were you? What was happening?

In Christ, we're born again. We can be like little children who have never been wounded by the big, bad scary world. Children who know our Dad is going to protect us. We can be like that because we are that.

If you've never considered that pride might be a big part of your anxiety, confess ways in which your heart has been prideful in the space below. It's hard to confess sin because it requires humility. But remember 1 John 1:9 says, "If we confess our sins, he is faithful and righteous to forgive us our sins and to cleanse us from all unrighteousness." And James 4:6 reminds us that God "gives grace to the humble."

Jesus isn't in the business of taking birds or saws away. He's a lover of souls and a lifter of burdens. When we communicate with Him through prayer, remembering the reality that He has that kind of power, we can echo Grandma Marlene (with the correct lyrics), singing, "I'm so happy and here's the reason why; Jesus took my burdens all away. . . ."[4]

DAY TWO
WEIRD NOSE-MOUTH-
LIP-FINGER SEASON

Philippians 4:1-9

The first six months after I had my thyroid removed, my body freaked out a little. Weird stuff started happening. For example, I had a photo album saved on my phone titled, "Weird nose mouth lip finger thing" that I brought to doctors' offices all over Nashville.

I don't want to gross you out, but there was ample oozing and swelling and crusting involved. ON MY FACE. Itching and tingling and burning. Is that enough? I'm sensing that you, reading this in the future, are uncomfortable. I'll stop. After just one more descriptor—gook.

So I'd just gone through the thyroid ordeal. I'd had blood tests and CT scans and all sorts of testing. So I guess I should have taken solace in that. But, in my mind, every throat tickle and allergic reaction was a symptom of something bigger. A sniffle is never just a sniffle with me. A sniffle is nasal cancer. An itch is lymphoma. A stomachache is clearly internal bleeding.

Toward the end of my weird nose mouth lip finger thing (WNMLFT from now on), I saw a specialist and described my symptoms. I showed him photos of all the sores, and I gave him a detailed timeline of events. When I was finished, he said, "Some of the words you used to describe your condition . . . are you in the medical field?"

Here's the point I'm getting at: what you put into your mind—what you think on—what you pray for—matters. I spent so much time worrying about being sick that I sounded like a doctor.

Maybe you already have this week's key sentence down. Maybe prayer is already your posture as you fight your anxiety. But if your prayers sound like mine did during WNMLFT season, you might find yourself remaining anxious, even as you pray.

During WNMLFT, my prayers were extremely similar to all the words I typed into *WebMD's* Symptom Checker. It was kind of like:

God, does the tip of my tongue feel numb? Lord, why is it so smooth here and bumpy there? Is that normal? Isn't it supposed to be bumpy in all areas? And my ring finger on the left hand has been itchy for way more than a week. That can't be normal, right, God? Let's You and I see what Google has to say about this for the next two hours.

I don't know that I ever got to the "Amen" because my prayers weren't really prayers as much as they were obsessively-fearful-brainstorming sessions.

What you think on matters.

Read Philippians 4:1-9. What are some words in verse 1 that let you know how the author (Paul) felt about the people he was writing to?

I point out that introduction because it is helpful as we apply the gospel to this passage. In the past, I've often attributed a tone to God's Word that just isn't there. This passage is not angry and obstinate. It's loving and helpful.

The Book of Philippians is Paul's letter to the people of Philippi, but it's also God's Word to us, today. God is not attacking us in this chapter for not thinking on the right things. He's lovingly helping us, just as Paul did with the Philippians, to think on the things that will bring life to our souls.

Read verses 4-7 again. What are the four things Paul said to do in these verses?

Which of these four things are you best at? Which do you need the most growth in?

In this letter, Paul was speaking to a church that was in the midst of persecution. So the "worry" these people were dealing with was valid, life-or-death fears.

Have you ever feared persecution for your beliefs? If so, what triggered that fear? If not, how do you feel when you consider persecuted Christians in the world today?

Look back at verse 9. What did Paul say is a result of following his instruction?

It's much harder to fear the broken, sad, and scariness of this world when you are experiencing the tangible presence of the more-powerful-than-ANYTHING God. Praying places your mind on God, and, when your mind is on God, your mind is on peace.

This next exercise might take you some time, but it will be worth it. Use Google (don't get side-tracked on *WebMD*) or a Bible dictionary to look up each of the terms in the chart. Then, write down something in each category that you are grateful for in the blanks beside the terms and back up your answers with a Bible reference. In the third blank, write down what that means for your battle with anxiety. I'll do the first one to give you an example.

	THING TO THINK ON	REFERENCE	WHAT THAT MEANS AS I FIGHT
WHAT IS TRUE?	"I am the way, truth, and the life."	John 14:6	Jesus is the Word, and His words are true, so when I'm afraid, I can remember that if He promises me hope and sharing in His glory for all eternity, I can be comforted by that.
WHAT IS HONORABLE?			
WHAT IS JUST?			
WHAT IS PURE?			

	THING TO THINK ON	REFERENCE	WHAT THAT MEANS AS I FIGHT
WHAT IS LOVELY?			
WHAT IS COMMENDABLE?			
WHAT IS MORALLY EXCELLENT?			
WHAT IS PRAISEWORTHY?			

Close out this day thanking Jesus for the blessings you listed. Ask Him to help your prayers be more worshipful and less doubting, more grateful and less anxious.

Oh, and by the way, it turns out WNMLFT was just an allergy to chapstick.

DAY THREE
WORLD'S MOST AMAZING PENCIL SHARPENER

MATTHEW 6:1-8

I don't know how extreme your teen angst was when you were in high school, but mine went deep. Pretty much everything I did in ninth grade was an effort to be seen/noticed/respected/admired by, well, every male that existed.

I remember sitting in my third hour class, making intense listening faces during lectures, asking the teacher what I considered to be thoughtful or funny or interesting questions, and getting up to sharpen my pencil with these thoughts in mind: *Are any of the three to seven boys that I'm in love with in this room looking at me, and, if so, are they daydreaming about how they will propose to me when I'm finished sharpening this pencil? And, if they do propose, what will I say? And if they ALL propose, whom will I choose?*

As you can tell, my early ideas about love were were very much about, um, me. I was so extremely wrapped up in my desire to be loved that I didn't love other people very well. My whole life was some sort of weird performance art that was, with zero subtlety saying, *LOOK AT ME! LOVE ME! PLEASE, I BEG OF YOU!*

I was also the kid who volunteered to close nearly every class in prayer at my Christian school. Because, I mean, then the teachers and even GOD would love me more, right?

I was a classic example of what Jesus said not to do in today's passage.

READ MATTHEW 6:1-8.

What did Jesus tell His disciples not to do in verses 1-4?

Is there anything you do in life for the sole purpose of being noticed/praised?

Those first few verses we just read were about generosity—helping the poor and doing good. But the next few we're going to look at are specifically about prayer.

Reread verses 5-8. What do you think Jesus meant when He said that the hypocrites who love to pray in public have their reward?

A lot of us are wired to look for reassurance that we're doing things the right way. There's no anxiety quite like the anxiety that comes with wondering if you got what matters for ETERNITY right. These verses are a gentle reminder to me that prayer isn't a formula to earn something. Prayer is its own reward.

What do the following verses tell you about the benefits of prayer?

2 Chronicles 7:14

Psalm 107:28-30

Psalm 145:18

Jeremiah 33:3

Matthew 7:7-8

Acts 9:40

Romans 8:26

Philippians 4:6-7

James 1:5

James 5:16

1 John 5:14-15

People who pray falsely for attention don't get the reward of friendship, intimacy, and actual, experiential, back-and-forth conversation with their Creator. There's nothing more incredible, nothing more peace-giving, nothing more worth your time, than talking to God in secret.

Describe the best prayer time you can remember experiencing.

What are some practical ways you can organize your schedule and life to make time and space for one-on-one alone time with God in prayer?

Examine yourself today. Are you still walking up to pencil sharpeners, anxious to be approved by fellow flawed people? You don't need to impress Jesus with your words or actions or pencil-sharpening-prowess. You're loved because you're His. You're forgiven because He's merciful. Dwell on that today in your thoughts, in your prayers, and in your deeds.

DAY FOUR
THE WORST PRAYER
I EVER PRAYED

Matthew 6:9–13; Matthew 11:28–30 and Romans 8:26–27

The worst prayer I ever prayed was on an operating room table. I was about to have the surgery that would save my life after an ectopic pregnancy left me with no baby, a quart of blood loose in my abdomen, and the worst pain I've ever felt.

The medical staff went from ultrasounding me to sprinting with my gurney in a single second. Papers that said things like "DNR" and "living will" were being shuffled near me, and nurses kept covering me with heated blankets because my teeth were chattering. I was going into shock.

When they transferred me from the gurney to the operating table, a stranger said, "Okay, I want you to count backwards from ten," and I knew I had less than ten seconds to tell God what might be my last words.

Silently, I prayed, *If I should die before I wake, I pray the Lord my soul to take . . .* [5]

What a tragedy. I'd been trying to walk with the Lord for a decade at that point, and my rhyme-y childhood prayer revealed that I was still anxious about my eternal security. Back then I'd had ten years of studying the Bible, praying, trying to pursue the things of the Lord, and, still, I wanted to just MAKE SURE if I'd "done it wrong" all those other times, I'd still make it into heaven.

God used that near-death tragedy in my life to give me assurance of my faith. And that prayer itself is an example of how that works.

Here's the beautiful thing. My worst prayer ever didn't change God's love for me. I could have sung my doubting nursery rhyme, died on the table, and woke up in His arms. It is not our skill that makes prayer powerful. It's the God we pray to. The weakest prayers have worth when we are children of God. And, amazingly, our Father not only makes prayer powerful, He helps us know how to do it.

Can you think of a time you prayed a "weak" prayer? What was happening? What about your prayer makes you consider it "weak"?

Read Matthew 6:9-13. Use it as a model and write your own prayer, verse by verse. For example, I might rewrite verse 9 ("Our Father in heaven, your name be honored as holy") by saying, "God, you are so much higher and bigger than I am. You are good and pure and clean and so different than me.")

Your Version:

Verse 9 _____

Verse 10 _____

Verse 11 _____

Verse 12 _____

Verse 13 _____

The Lord's Prayer here might sound very formal, but the point of Matthew 6 is that God doesn't want you to pray or talk or act to perform. Because of Jesus, God is our Dad. Because of Jesus, we don't have to feel guilty when we talk to Him.

I look at this prayer to help me when I'm not sure how I should pray. It reminds me to thank God for who He is and what He's done, rather than grow desensitized and forgetful. It teaches me I am fully dependent on Him to meet my every need.

Reread Matthew 6:9-13. What does Jesus' example of prayer teach you?

Remember what God does in our weakness? Review Romans 8:26-27. What does He do?

Here's a thing. I don't think God considered my "worst prayer" to be the worst. I don't think that's true, based on what I know of Jesus.

Flip to Matthew 11:28-30. What did Jesus say in these verses?

Isn't that crazy? Jesus is humble. Jesus is the only being who doesn't NEED to be humble!

He and the Father are one. But He lowers Himself. He associates with us, sinners. He has compassion for our weaknesses. We can pray weak prayers. We can pray silent prayers. We can pray frustrated or sad or joyful prayers.

Jesus loves us. It's that simple. And He knows it's hard to talk to someone we can't see. So He gives us this beautiful example. This beautiful reminder.

Close this day out thanking Him for showing us the way and for loving us when we do it wrong or when we feel too weak or anxious to do it at all. Ask Him to transform your prayer life and help you learn to pray in a way that glorifies Him and helps your heart toward peace.

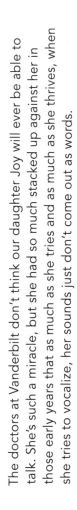

DAY FIVE
JOY'S SECRET LANGUAGE

Matthew 10:22; John 10:10; John 15:18–27 and Romans 8:18–28

The doctors at Vanderbilt don't think our daughter Joy will ever be able to talk. She's such a miracle, but she had so much stacked up against her in those early years that as much as she tries and as much as she thrives, when she tries to vocalize, her sounds just don't come out as words.

People can't understand her.

It's something that was way harder to deal with at first. When we weren't all fluent in sign language, it would kill me to not know what she was saying. Sometimes she'd cry and get upset and make noises, and none of us could figure out what they meant.

Now, she signs, and we usually get it, but once in a while, we're all left scratching our heads, and she usually shrugs and signs, "Never mind—it was nothing," and she walks away.

It's a hard thing. It's a hard thing for her; I'm sure. And it's a hard thing, as her parent, to want to connect and understand what she's thinking and not be able to. Maybe you've experienced something similar when trying to communicate with someone who doesn't speak your language.

We humans, even those of us without any physical or mental special needs, are limited in our communication. Have you ever been speechless? Even people with the most sophisticated vocabularies sometimes find themselves in situations where they just don't have the words.

Read Romans 8:18-28. Which of these verses means the most to you today and why?

In verses 18-22, Paul reflected on how much different it will be when we are free from suffering, free from "labor pains" (v. 22). Can you even imagine it? During my most intense seasons of anxiety, my mind has made me feel like the suffering would never end.

What is a circumstance about which you "groan within" yourself (v. 23) today? What do you look forward to being relieved from?

Read John 10:10 and copy the second sentence in the space below.

For Christians, it can be tempting to look at today's passage and feel hopeless about today and like everything will be pins and needles and the wringing of hands until heaven. The gospel tells us this isn't true, though.

If you've been part of the church for a while, you may have heard the term *abundant life* thrown around. That term comes from this verse, when Jesus was explaining He has come so we can have life in abundance.

Some people misinterpret this and think Jesus is saying if you follow Him, you'll have all the good stuff of life. In reality, Jesus promised otherwise.

Read Matthew 10:22 and John 15:18-27. How did Jesus say our lives as followers of Him would be?

Life can be hard and still be abundant. Jesus told His disciples and is telling us now that joyful life is from Him. Life in abundance is only found when we pursue Him and His kingdom. Anything and everything else will leave us anxious and unsatisfied.

Have you tested that truth? Have you pursued peace and pleasure in things outside of Jesus and found they didn't work?

Share below about the things your flesh craves and where those roads lead.

So we pray. We pray, remembering the truth of Romans 8. We pray, remembering the truth of Jesus as our way to life and peace. We pray, remembering the reality that after this life, we will someday be in actual glory with everlasting peace that can never go anywhere. We pray that way, and it changes us right now.

We pray that way, and the casting of cares and releasing of burdens actually happens.

One day, my youngest asked me if Joy would be able to talk in heaven. It got me emotional. I'd never considered it. My communication with my non-verbal daughter is limited. But Philippians 3:21 tells me that at Christ's return, we'll get new bodies. Perfect ones where all the parts work and we won't fear them breaking down anymore. And Joy's ears and mouth will work. And we'll never wonder what she's saying as she praises her Maker with us around the throne.

What are you grateful for right now? Tell God about it. He's listening.

This past week, you completed the Session Six personal study in your books. If you weren't able to do so, no big deal! You can still follow along with the questions, be involved in the discussion, and watch the video. When you are ready to begin, open up your time in prayer and push play on Video Six for Session Six.

WATCH

Write down any thoughts, verses, or things you want to remember as you watch the video for Session Six of Anxious.

REVIEW SESSION SIX PERSONAL STUDY

From Day One: What are some practical ways you can "humble yourself" before God?

From Day Two: In Philippians 4:4-7, what four things did Paul say to do?

From Day Three: What are some practical ways you can organize your schedule and life to make time and space for one-on-one alone time with God in prayer?

From Day Four: What does Jesus' example of prayer teach you?

From Day Five: Which of the verses that you looked at from Romans 8 means the most to you this week and why?

FROM THIS WEEK'S STUDY

As a group, review this week's memory verse.

Humble yourselves, therefore, under the mighty hand of God, so that he may exalt you at the proper time, casting all your cares on him, because he cares about you.

1 PETER 5:6-7

DISCUSS

This week, we studied prayer. We talked about how to do it, how not to do it, and how we can cast our cares on Jesus. If you're comfortable with it, discuss your own experience with prayer. In which ways do you struggle? What are some disciplines you have put in your life to help you? Do you have any amazing stories of answered prayer?

What is one thing you have been anxious about this week? How can this group pray for you?

This session's main idea is "Prayer is our posture in the fight against anxiety." Are there any ways you now intend to pray differently when taking your burdens to the Lord? Discuss ideas with your group.

PRAY

This would be a great week to use most of your time to pray for one another. Consider praying through the Lord's Prayer (Matt. 6:9-13) together. Maybe take one verse at a time and add to it in the direction Jesus leads. Look back to Day Four and see how you changed each verse's example into your own words. Take turns praying like this and for one another's burdens.

To access the teaching sessions, use the instructions in the back of your Bible study book.

ANXIOUS READER

THE BIBLE IS OUR WEAPON IN
THE FIGHT AGAINST ANXIETY

[THE ORDINANCES OF
THE LORD] ARE MORE
DESIRABLE THAN GOLD—
THAN AN ABUNDANCE OF
PURE GOLD; AND SWEETER
THAN HONEY DRIPPING
FROM A HONEYCOMB. IN
ADDITION, YOUR SERVANT
IS WARNED BY THEM, AND
IN KEEPING THEM THERE IS
AN ABUNDANT REWARD.

Psalm 19:10–11

DAY ONE
SO HOW'S LEVITICUS GOING FOR YA?

Hebrews 4:1–12

In 2008, a friend and I decided we were going to hold each other accountable to read through the Bible from Genesis to Revelation in one year.

It was a good goal to set, and the first few days of texting back and forth went really well.

The thing is, we both dropped off. One of us missed a day. One of us had a crisis. The texts stopped. The plan was thwarted. We never finished it.

I write this in the year 2020 and smile because every few years, she and I will check in with a text: "So . . . what are you on now . . . Leviticus?

Bible reading can be hard. The Bible was written in different languages across years and years to multiple audiences. It contains books like Leviticus and Revelation. Add to that complexity the reality that we have an enemy who comes "only to steal and kill and destroy" (John 10:10), and it should be no surprise that there are days Bible reading seems like work.

But the Bible isn't just a book from history; it is a book from heaven (Ps. 119:89). It doesn't just have old words; it has God's words (2 Tim. 3:16). It isn't just long; it is alive (1 Pet. 1:23). The Bible literally does supernatural work in your heart while you read it (Isa. 55:11).

Our own weakness, anxiety, selfishness, and sin, at times, make the Bible hard to read, but it is light and life itself (Ps. 119:130; Matt. 4:4). The Bible is our weapon as we fight to trust God and find the peace He gives.

What are some of the most common reasons you don't read your Bible?

I'll answer that question as well. One of the primary reasons I will ignore the Bible is because I sometimes bring my anxiousness filter into the text.

When my anxiety is fierce, I find I can misread Scripture and, instead of a loving God with an easy yoke, I see a judging One with a list of demands I can never adhere to. God's plan for us is peace, but it is possible to read the Bible and panic.

Read Hebrews 4:1-12. What does your heart and mind latch onto when you look at verse 1?

This is a great example of how anxiety can impact the reading of Scripture. Some of you probably saw "the promise to enter his rest remains" (v. 1) and thought Yeeeeeeees.

Others of you saw, "beware that none of you be found to have fallen short" (v. 1) and thought, I'm dooooomed.

Which reaction did you have? (Feel free to add your own write-in reaction. I've given you an extra box.)

○ *Yeeeeeeees.*
○ *I'm dooooomed.*
○ _____

Both phrases are true. Here in Hebrews 4 is the hope of rest, as well as a warning about unbelief. It can be pretty scary to read if you're used to listening to the lies your anxiety tells you. But the perfect love of Christ "casts out fear" (1 John 4:18, ESV), so let's look, soberly, at this text and examine our hearts—not in a panic but as children of God.

Look at Hebrews 4:2–4.

What keeps people from entering the rest?

What are some things you do when you're trying to rest?

The Lord, the One who invented rest (see verse 4) when He created everything you know and see, knows how to satisfy your soul. He knows how to give you peace because He invented peace.

Our Hebrews 4 passage deals with several types of rest, among them are—ultimate rest in salvation, eternal enjoyment in heaven, and peace that we can experience even now on earth through Christ's provision.

How does the eternal rest promised by God through salvation in this passage form the way that you can rest your anxious heart even in the here and now?

Entering into the rest can be as easy as entering into His presence. If God's Word is alive and true and made to lead you to Him, time in God's Word should be a comfort, not a chore.

Now look back at verse 10. When we imitate God by resting, what is it that we are resting from?

It's exhausting trying to do everything right, isn't it? Because we fail! Eventually our working turns to worrying turns to wandering away. And if our hope and our peace and our rest is all tied up in us "doing good," we will be crushed when we have a bad day.

Reread verse 11. Rather than pursuing our own goodness, what does God's Word tell us to make an effort to do?

In verse 12, what are some things we learn the Word of God is able to do?

Isn't it crazy that a book can read your mind? I mean, it sounds crazy until you remember that the Bible is inspired, or "God-breathed." If God's Word is alive and active in that book, He is certainly able to know you and speak to you, shape you and teach you through those words. It's such a beautiful truth.

My friend and I or your friends and you can plan to try to read through the Bible in a year or three months or a weekend. And maybe you'll do it! But if you're doing it to earn God's approval, to check a box, or to stay out of hell (that was me), you're missing the rest. You're missing the magic. You're missing the gift that God's Word is to our anxious hearts. God wants you to read His Word and enter His rest here on earth and eternally.

Close out this day by thanking God for His Word, this gift, this weapon. In your prayer, reflect on a time God's Word was a weapon in your fight against fear, if one comes to mind.

DAY TWO
"GOOD PEOPLE" AND BIBLE READING

Psalm 19:1–11

Here's some of what I battle when it comes to Bible reading:

- I get anxious about "doing it right" or "doing it enough," and I forget that it is a living, active gift.

- I get distracted thinking about using the wrong kind of Bible. Do super Christians read the Bible on their phones? That's not as good, right? I need a big, worn study Bible. I need a Bible that doesn't have the Tiny Wings™ app on it. Man, Tiny Wings is great. Can you believe your daughter has gotten better than you at Tiny Wings? Unacceptable, Scarlet. Be better. Just be better. We're going to practice Tiny Wings today, and we will absolutely win the race to Island 4 tonight.

- I get anxious/frustrated when I read things I don't understand.

- I focus so much on potential dangers or problems I feel like I need to fix that I fail to look to the Lord.

It takes discipline to read the Bible regularly and well. What sort of rhythms have you put in place in your life to help you stay consistent?

Reading the Bible doesn't have to be a battle. Today, we're going to look at the first part of a psalm David wrote, and we'll reflect on what it tells us about the Bible. But first, let's look at the beginning of this psalm.

Read Psalm 19:1-6. In these verses, what is it that is declaring and proclaiming the glory of God?

General revelation is the phrase used to explain how God's glory and character are revealed to mankind through nature.[1] It's that thing when you stand at the ocean, speechless. The thing when you see a baby being born or you stand on top of a mountain or look out over a valley and just think, Wow.

The natural world tells us God is glorious. Creation, in its scope and life, reveals some of the beauty and grandeur of God.

But God doesn't leave us staring at trees and "Wowing" at seas while wondering what it all means.

Read Psalm 19:7-11.

Special revelation is supernatural communication between God and humanity.[2] Verses 7-11 are speaking directly to that.

What key words in this passage tell us these verses are about the Bible?

What words did David use in verses 7 and 8 to describe the Bible?

Read verse 11. What did David mean when he said, "in keeping them there is great reward" (ESV)?

When I was a teenager, I'd leave to hang out with my friends or go on a date, and my dad would stop me and say, "Scarlet, remember, all sin leads to heartache." He said that so many times.

He was giving me freedom. Freedom to go sit in movie theaters or go to parties with other seventeen year olds. But, a warning. His warning wasn't, "Don't do bad stuff, or I'll ground you." His warning was, "If you sin, you will hurt. I love you, and I don't want you to hurt."

That's what the Bible does for us so often! It is like God, leaning over the kitchen counter, saying, "This is how to live, child! Remember, sin leads to heartache."

The reward of "keeping" God's Word as a priority in your life is peace—joy—happiness! He doesn't give us rules to harm us. He gives us instruction to protect us. He is a good Father.

In the space below, write out some personal reasons you treasure God's Word.

DAY THREE
A LETTER WE CAN
LEARN FROM

Matthew 16:25 and 2 Timothy 3:10-17

Paul, the apostle, (the guy who was also known as Saul—a serious big-time Jew who killed Christians, but then Jesus blinded him and revealed Himself and then he spent the rest of his life serving and preaching and writing Bible books—that guy) . . . well, let me just stop and take a breath. I'm just really proud of myself for that summary of Paul's life.

If you want the non-abridged version, read about his amazing conversion story in Acts 9.

Moving on. Paul wrote a bunch of Bible books—letters to churches and to people—letters that were written then and for then but that God designed to be applied to us today.

Author and Bible teacher Jen Wilkin did an Instagram Q&A, and I loved what she said about applying Scripture. She said, "All Scripture applies first to its original audience . . . This is important because how we apply it today must relate to how they applied it then. It can't mean something to us that it could never have meant to them then. Once you examine what it said to them-for-then, think about its message to us-for-always."[3]

So first, let's look at the "then" context of our 2 Timothy passage. Paul was writing this letter to Timothy, whom he met during a missionary journey.

In the chapter we're looking at today, he was encouraging Timothy not to lose heart during times of stress and suffering.

Read 2 Timothy 3:10-17.

What was Paul reflecting on in verses 10 and 11?

Who did Paul credit for his rescue from troubles?

What are some difficult circumstances you've endured recently?

Are you able to echo Paul in any similar ways? How did the Lord provide for you?

Reread verses 12-13. What did Paul say all who want to live a godly life will experience?

I used to get so caught up in verses like these. I'd think, NO THANK YOU. I WANT A GOOD LIFE. But I've lived plenty of seasons of "good life" and still been miserable.

I've lived fearful I'd lose what I had. Stressed over things that didn't matter. We can get caught up fearing the bad stuff of this life when we forget that we have a prize that can't be taken from us.

We think if we cling to the things we love in life, we'll save them. But the opposite is actually true.

Read Matthew 16:25.

What did Jesus say will happen to someone who gets caught up in "sav[ing] his life"?

Then, Jesus went on to describe a group that will find life. What are believers to do with their lives, according to Jesus?

If we are anxious to cling to anything in life other than Jesus, we'll find that we're never at peace. No matter how good we are at worrying, we aren't capable of holding on to anything. We don't have the power to keep life going and to keep jobs safe and to keep bodies healthy. When we "lose" our lives or surrender them, when we trust that Jesus knows better than we do, there is where we find the peace.

Read 2 Timothy 3:14–17.

What did Paul say Scripture gives us (v. 15)?

I love verses 16 and 17 so much. What a beautiful list of benefits. In the chart below, I want you to take each benefit and write down in the blank how that specific thing can help you as you fight your anxiety.

Teaching _____

Rebuking _____

Correcting _____

Training in
Righteousness _____

The Bible teaches us about the God who died to free us from slavery to fear. The Bible rebukes us when we are numb to sin and indulging in self-centeredness. The Bible corrects us when we look to the wrong things for comfort and security. The Bible trains us to live lives centered on enjoying the love we have in Christ and sharing it with others. The Bible reminds us that to lose our lives is to find our lives.

It really does equip us. It equips us to be happy, healthy children. It prepares us to be ambassadors—service-minded, fulfilled, contented people who bring their burdens to the only One who is strong enough to carry them.

Close this day asking the Lord what He wants to speak into your life in regard to your fears today. Ask Him. Read. Listen. Write it down below. Remember it. God is for You. He loves you. His Word is a gift and a weapon.

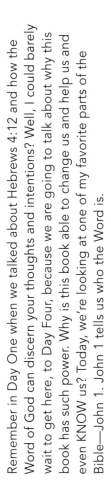

DAY FOUR
THE WORD IS A PERSON

Genesis 1:26; Matthew 24:35; Luke 21:33 and John 1:1-5,14

Remember in Day One when we talked about Hebrews 4:12 and how the Word of God can discern your thoughts and intentions? Well, I could barely wait to get here, to Day Four, because we are going to talk about why this book has such power. Why is this book able to change us and help us and even KNOW us? Today, we're looking at one of my favorite parts of the Bible—John 1. John 1 tells us who the Word is.

Read John 1:1-5. What do we learn about "the Word" from these verses?

Now, look down the Bible page to verse 14. If the Word is God, and the Word was made flesh and dwelt among us, who is the Word?

Commentator James Montgomery Boice wrote,

What do you think of Jesus Christ? Who is he? According to Christianity this is the most important question you or anyone else will ever have to face. It is important because it is inescapable—you will have to answer it sooner or later, in this world or in the world to come—and because the quality of your life here and your eternal destiny depend upon your answer. Who is Jesus Christ? If he was only a man, then you can safely forget him. If he is God, as he claimed to be, and as all Christians believe, then you should yield your life to him. You should worship and serve him faithfully.[4]

The reality that Jesus is God isn't just a fact you have to memorize to excel at the Christian faith. It's the basis of our faith. If Jesus isn't God, then we aren't forgiven. If Jesus isn't God, we still await punishment for our sins. If Jesus isn't God, we have no access to our Creator, no access to the joy we can only find in His presence, and no access to eternal life beyond the grave.

Jesus is God. Jesus has always been God and will always be God. But Jesus isn't only described as God. Jesus is "the Word." Jesus, our Rescuer, our Hope, our Peace, is alive in the pages of Scripture.

Now, look at Genesis 1:26. Are there any words in this verse that lead you to believe God the Father wasn't alone when He created the world? List them here.

John 1:2-3 affirms Jesus was there with God the Father, in the beginning. So in this little handful of verses, we learn that Jesus is called the Word.

We learn He is God—that He also, as God, created all things. Listen, maybe that makes your brain hurt. No problem. Just thank God He is smarter than us!

But it's really important as we seek to worship Jesus to recognize He isn't just a guy, and He isn't even "just" God. Jesus is revealed to us in the Bible. God is speaking through those pages.

Have you ever been reading the Bible and experienced Jesus? (By that, I mean, have you ever been reading the Bible and felt you were not just reading a book about God but that you were communicating *with* God through the power of the Holy Spirit?)

What are some specific passages He has used in your life? Share about them in the space below.

Look up Matthew 24:35 and Luke 21:33. What do these accounts tell us Jesus said?

Isn't it comforting to know that Jesus created us, that He is forever, that no matter what comes against them, His words are forever too? When you hear them, when you read them, when you commit them to memory, the Spirit stirs in your soul and helps you believe the truth—the truth that this scary world isn't forever, but Jesus is.

What is the most recent thing you've done when you felt overcome by panic?

Sometimes, I wake up in a panic. Maybe it's a bad dream, or, often, I just wake up to get water and a horrible thought crosses my mind. What if such and such happened to my husband? What if one of my daughters does this or that? What if-what if-what if-what if . . .

Often, I lie back down and either think of the Word or read the Word, or sometimes I just whisper the Word's name, "Jesus."

But if you only have one word, that's the one. He is the One. He is the Word.

Take the next few minutes to look through my list of favorite anxiety-fighting memory verses in the Appendix on pages 186–187. Pick out a verse that will give you some words to carry with you for the rest of the day. Write out the verse you picked that reminds you how loved and protected you are by the Prince of peace in the space below and try to memorize it.

If you read the Bible and don't experience Jesus, examine your heart and ask yourself what your motives are.

Try to answer these next few questions honestly by checking the one that best fits your response.

When you open the Bible, are you looking to experience God, or are you trying to "do what good people do"?

○ Looking to experience God.

○ Trying to do what good people do.

When you read the Bible, do you open it randomly and pull verses out not knowing what they mean and then close it, feeling like you've done your duty for the day?

○ Yes.

○ Nah, not my style.

If you don't understand something you've read, do you give up, or do you press in and research what it means?

○ Throw in the towel.

○ Research is my middle name.

A lot of our Bible frustrations exist because we forget that God meets us when we open the Bible. We read it because we should. Or we read it because that makes us feel like we're winning at life. Don't read the Bible like you're completing a homework assignment you don't want to do. Read it like you're on a coffee date with your best friend and what you're reading is what He's saying (and what He's saying are the words of life). Go to the Bible like what you're reading is His advice to you, His encouragement to you, His comfort for you.

Now, write out a prayer, worshiping and thanking God for giving us access to Himself through His Word.

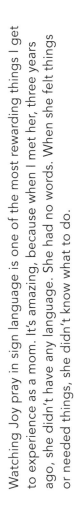

DAY FIVE
WATCHING JOY PRAY

John 17:1-19

Watching Joy pray in sign language is one of the most rewarding things I get to experience as a mom. It's amazing, because when I met her, three years ago, she didn't have any language. She had no words. When she felt things or needed things, she didn't know what to do.

For a week and a half, while still in China, we actually didn't think she'd ever learn any words. She was so medically not ok. But our first glimmer of hope came at the buffet table when she realized that every time Daddy fed her a bite of vanilla yogurt, it was after he brought her fingers to her lips. The sign for *food*.

Next, she learned the word *drink*. Then, *cracker*. Sweet Joy was hungry. And those three words changed her life.

Now, she prays.

This week, I had a tooth pulled (my teeth hate me), and before I left for the dentist, I told the girls I was a little scared. My oldest offered to pray for me, and it was so precious. And then, Joy took over. She squeezed her eyes shut, and her hand went to work praying for every detail of what I was about to experience. She prayed that I wouldn't be afraid.

Read John 17:1-19.

In John 17:1-19, we read about Jesus, the Word made flesh, praying for His disciples. Two times in His prayer, He made requests in connection to the Word. What were those two requests?

In verse 13, Jesus desired for His disciples to have completed joy. Write about a time you have obeyed God's Word and felt joy.

In verse 17, Jesus asked that God sanctify His friends through the Word. Let's give this some attention. Look up the word *sanctify* in a dictionary and write out the definition below.

To be *sanctified* is to be separated from things that are evil, things that are not pleasing to God. When we talk about being sanctified, we are talking about living as followers of Christ. So, naturally, we see plenty of instruction about how Christians are to live in the Word.

We're not going to walk perfectly. But to be sanctified means to take steps of obedience and pursue the Lord through prayer and through His Word. That is how we become like Him. That is how we experience the joy of verse 13. This is how we learn to be less anxious people. The Word leads us toward sanctification and away from anxiety.

Think back to the most peaceful season of your life. What were you doing? What was happening?

Where were you in your relationship with Christ?

One of the most peaceful seasons of my life was when we were in the adoption process. We didn't have the money to do what we were doing. We didn't have medical answers or even hope that things would work out at all. But we knew we were walking the direction the Lord was leading. His Word comforted us when we were sad. It convicted us out of our fears. It humbled us when we forgot He was the only reason anything good ever happens to us.

Why does it matter that Jesus asked God to sanctify His friends through the Word? Because, essentially, what He was asking was that His friends would be safe—have peace—be happy. Safety, peace, and happiness are the opposites of anxiety. And God wants that for us. God wants that for you.

Copy this week's memory verse (found at the beginning of this lesson) in the margin. (I've shown you where). →

Now, let's look back at the memory verses we've already learned. See if you can fill in the blanks from memory without looking back. God's Word is a weapon. His Word is a comfort. His Word is a way to fight anxiety. Praise God.

SESSION TWO

Many say about me, "There is no _____ for him in God." *Selah.* But you, LORD, are a _____ around me, my _____, and the one who _____ up _____.

PSALM 3:2-3

SESSION THREE

But seek _____ the kingdom of God and

his _____, and all these things will

be _____ for you. Therefore _____

about tomorrow, because tomorrow will worry

about itself. Each day has enough _____ of its own.

MATTHEW 6:33-34

SESSION FOUR

But Moses said to the people, "Don't be _____.

Stand _____ and see the LORD's _____

that _____ will _____ for you today; for the

Egyptians you see today, you will never see again. The

LORD _____ for you, and you must be _____."

EXODUS 14:13-14

SESSION FIVE

If you keep _____ at this time, relief and

will come to the Jewish people _____ another

_____, but you and your father's family will be

destroyed. Who knows, _____ you have come to

your royal position for _____ a _____ as _____.

ESTHER 4:14

SESSION SIX

_____ yourselves, therefore, under the

_____ hand of _____, so that he may exalt

you at the _____ time, _____ all your _____

on _____, because he _____ about you.

1 PETER 5:6-7

This past week, you completed the Session Seven personal study in your books. If you weren't able to do so, no big deal! You can still follow along with the questions, be involved in the discussion, and watch the video. When you are ready to begin, open up your time in prayer and push play on Video Seven for Session Seven.

WATCH

Write down any thoughts, verses, or things you want to remember as you watch the video for Session Seven of Anxious.

FROM THIS WEEK'S STUDY

As a group, review this week's memory verse.

[The ordinances of the LORD] are more desirable than gold—than an abundance of pure gold; and sweeter than honey dripping from a honeycomb. In addition, your servant is warned by them, and in keeping them there is an abundant reward.

PSALM 19:10-11

REVIEW SESSION SEVEN PERSONAL STUDY

From Day One: What are some of the most common reasons you don't read your Bible?

According to Hebrews 4:2-4, what keeps people from entering the rest?

From Day Two: What sort of rhythms have you put in place in your life to help you stay consistent with your Bible reading?

From Day Three: What are some of the benefits of Scripture, as found in 2 Timothy 3:16-17?

From Day Four: Have you ever been reading the Bible and experienced Jesus? (By that, I mean, have you ever been reading the Bible and felt you were not just reading a book about God but that you were communicating with God through the power of the Holy Spirit?)

From Day Five: Think back to the most peaceful season of your life. What were you doing? What was happening? Where were you in your relationship with Christ?

DISCUSS

This week, we talked about fighting anxiety with the Word as our weapon. If you're comfortable sharing, discuss ways and circumstances in which you've used God's Word to fight your worries.

What are some ways you've struggled with your Bible reading? Since you're together as a group, this is a great opportunity for those of you who have walked with the Lord for a long time to share what has helped you in your pursuit of studying the Word.

Do you have a key Scripture passage you turn to when you're feeling afraid? Discuss that passage with your group.

Is there something you could do together as a group to hold each other accountable for time in the Word/Bible memorization? Brainstorm together.

PRAY

Today, challenge yourselves as a group to pray Scripture. Take five minutes to look through the Psalms or other parts of the Bible for some Scripture you can use in your prayer time together. Then spend the rest of the prayer time lifting up the needs of your group and asking God to help you as you encourage one another and fight, side by side, with the living and active Word as your weapon.

To access the teaching sessions, use the instructions in the back of your Bible study book.

ANXIOUS TOGETHER

COMMUNITY IS OUR LIFELINE IN
THE FIGHT AGAINST ANXIETY

AND LET US CONSIDER ONE
ANOTHER IN ORDER TO
PROVOKE **LOVE** AND **GOOD**
WORKS, NOT NEGLECTING
TO GATHER TOGETHER, AS
SOME ARE IN THE HABIT OF
DOING, BUT **ENCOURAGING**
EACH OTHER, AND ALL THE
MORE AS YOU SEE THE
DAY APPROACHING.

Hebrews 10:24-25

DAY ONE
MEDICAL SHOWS, SNACKS, AND PLEASE, NO PEOPLE

Hebrews 10:19-25

Shortly after my near-death ectopic pregnancy experience, I got pretty dark.

I couldn't return to work for a month because I couldn't move. I was married without any kids yet, and my husband had gone back to work, so all there was in my life that month was the TV medical dramas I binged on, the snacks I binged on, and the deep sadness I weirdly relished.

I wanted to be sad. I wanted to be distracted. I wanted the world to leave me alone.

I remember my small group trying to invite me back into civilization, and I remember ignoring their calls. I remember Super Bowl party invitations I threw away. And I remember staying home from church on Sundays, even when I was well enough to go.

I didn't want to hear people telling me God had a reason for this. I didn't want people to smile sympathetically and say, "When are you going to try for another baby?" I didn't want people encouraging me to pray. I didn't want any of it. I just wanted to escape with my *Grey's Anatomy*, *House*, and my bedside bag of Hot Tamales®.

Have you ever experienced a season of discouragement?

What were the circumstances, and what were you feeling?

I pushed people away. I pushed God away. I didn't want to fake-smile or fake-talk or fake-pray. I just wanted to be distracted from my sadness, and I thought the way to do that was to isolate myself.

Deep down, I was afraid to approach God with my feelings because I knew my feelings were misguided. It felt wrong to be mad at Him for the circumstances I was in. So I stayed silent. I stayed away. And my soul started to shrivel.

Read Hebrews 10:19-25. Because of Jesus, what does verse 22 say our hearts will be full of?

I think the enemy jumps at the opportunity when he sees a discouraged Christian. Since he can't take us out, he just tries to shut us out. If he can keep us from wanting to approach the throne of grace, he can keep us shriveling up.

The truth is, we can approach God with boldness, even if we're discouraged. Even if we're messed up and angry and at our worst. We can approach our Father and talk to Him and trust Him because of the blood of Jesus. (If this phrase is unfamiliar to you, flip over to pages 184–185 in the Appendix.)

Look again at verse 23.

Why is it that we can hold on to our confession of hope?

In the space below, write out your own confession of hope in a couple of sentences. What has Jesus done for you?

Read verses 24-25.

God created us for community. God created us to help each other and to remind each other that we have the same confession. What Christ did for one messed up, angry, sad, flawed human, He did for all of us. His sacrifice bought us access to the only One who can comfort us and heal us and assure us we are loved and okay, even when we don't feel like it.

He uses other believers to remind us of this.

Can you think of a time in your life when the body of Christ held you together when you were weak? Describe it below.

Sometimes anxiety doesn't look like being scared of bad things. Sometimes it looks like being afraid of God, being anxious about asking Him the hard questions and being worried about letting other people help us and love us and see us at our worst.

The community of other Christians is our lifeline in the fight against anxiety. I don't know how I would have crawled out of my TV and candy crises if it hadn't been for Brandi and Nicole bringing me meals, Pastor Rick telling me the disciples struggled with doubting Jesus too, Toni telling me I could tell God how I felt even if my feelings were painful, and Jackie praying and fasting on my behalf and being a non-judgmental ear when I said I didn't want to pray. Those people brought me back to life with Jesus.

What can you do this week to lean on other believers or let them lean on you?

DAY TWO
ON HATING HELPING
Acts 2:42-47

I've cycled through a lot of church-y anxieties. Maybe you can relate. I have often dreaded Sunday mornings in fear of:

- being asked to serve in children's ministry;

- being approached by eager, passionate mission trip leaders;

- being told unexpectedly that someone had a "word" for me (I'm not anti-"word," but it has, during anxious times, certainly caught me off guard).

I think, if you'd given me some sort of truth serum during the years I was a very young pastor's wife, I would have confessed something to the effect of, "I hate helping."

If you get anxious about other people placing expectations or demands on you, that's probably not something you'd like to admit on paper. So I won't ask the question, lest someone look over at your Bible study book when you're sharing answers. But I suspect you've sometimes felt the same way.

The church can, at times, feel like a steady stream of *DO MORE. HELP ME. GIVE THIS. BOY, DO I HAVE A CALLING FOR YOU.* At just the wrong time, it can send you over the edge.

As Christians, we want to please the Lord, so when we feel like we're not or feel like other people think we're not, it can lead us to run away from the people we need and the people who need us.

Let's compare this tendency to the activity of the early church.

Read Acts 2:42-47.

What were the early Christians devoted to?

How do these things compare to what you or the believers in your life are devoted to?

This next part is for those of you who are wired like me to read your own experiences and fears and failures into the text. Let me reassure you.

I don't want you to start breathing into a paper bag over this passage as I have in the past. We have to look at the cultural context of the early church. Just because they gathered daily doesn't mean you're out of the will of God if you don't have daily worship gatherings at your church.

On this note, Ajith Fernando wrote,

Nowhere is it stated that Christians should continue to meet daily as they did in the first days of the Jerusalem church (v. 46). Considering the responsibilities one has in family life and in witness and vocation in society, it may not be a good idea for Christians to have a program in church every day of the week. History has shown that usually at the start of a revival there are daily meetings. After that it tapers off into a less frequent but regular pattern. Certainly it is helpful for new believers to be with Christians daily until they are more stable in their faith.[1]

All this to say, breathe in and breathe out if your small group isn't on a daily schedule. Don't throw away your traditional church programming experience because of this text. The early church was a community. They ate together. They helped each other. They worshiped, side by side.

In our culture, this might look like texting the family in your small group to see if they need help organizing meals after a surgery. It might look like giving your bag of hand-me-down toddler clothes to the young family that shares one car. (We were that family and my daughters still wear those clothes—thank you, Beverly!) It looks like making attendance and participation in your local church a priority. Not because you will be punished if you don't, but because you will be loved and able to love and encourage others when you do!

Look at verses 46 and 47. What two adjectives describe the hearts of the people in this early church?

I remember reading Acts 2 when I was in the I-hate-helping phase of my life and thinking, OK, *this sounds terrible. I don't want to have people in my house/room/world. I don't want to give away my stuff. I want to eat nachos by myself, thank you.* (I actually still stand by that one. Eating nachos alone is the only way to eat nachos.)

Our inherent selfishness can lead us to believe we will feel peaceful if we're alone with our nachos, detached from people's drama. But in the Spirit, we have everything in common. When we learn to let go of our other-people-anxiety, we can actually experience things like JOY, sincere love, and peace.

Share about a time you experienced joy in being there for a brother or sister in Christ.

There's so much beauty in being dependent on each other. There's beauty in needing other believers. When we approach the Lord and one another with the humility that says, "I need Jesus, and I need you," we find that we're not alone. When we're scared, we're held together and surrounded by a body of believers who share our hope and remind us of our hope and embody our hope in their actions.

I'm happy to report I don't hate helping anymore. That's because as I got a little older and a little more world-weary, I discovered how much I needed help. I've experienced the deep need for the sincere love and generosity of other believers. I've known the joy of being weak when others who were strong in the body of Christ comforted me and restored me and led me back to the peace I have because I am held by Christ.

Close out this day praying for the people in your life that you might be used by the Lord to love them and comfort them and assure them they are loved and safe. Ask the Lord to help you have the courage to imitate the early church and become a person who loves helping and being helped.

DAY THREE

WOULD YOU RATHER CHANGE DIAPERS OR LEARN SIGN LANGUAGE?

John 13:34-35; 1 Corinthians 12:12-26 and Philippians 2:8

Being part of the body of Christ feels a little bit like playing that game "Would You Rather?"

One of my favorite church moments happened while discussing a sermon with some friends. We'd been meeting together for a while, and we were a smorgasbord of people. There was a couple in their twenties—the husband a Christian musician and the wife in nursing school. There was a single guy, an older married couple, and a handful of other people in varying life stages and situations. We didn't have a whole lot in common besides Jesus.

So this one day, we started discussing what our pastor had taught and what his message was encouraging us to pursue. We went around the circle sharing what we felt personally called to.

One person said she wanted to sign up to rock babies in the nursery on Sundays. A newlywed couple said they had a heart to foster middle school boys from troubled homes. We talked about the struggles of communication we were experiencing in our adoption. And after a few minutes of sharing, we all started laughing.

We all felt called to such different things, and not a single one of us wanted anything to do with what the person next to us felt called to.

It was a happy moment because we all realized we were being the body, as God intended it.

I remember my husband saying, "I would never, ever want to rock babies on Sundays. That is the last thing I would sign up to do." And whoever said that laughed and said, "Well, I don't know how you all adopted a deaf daughter. That sounds impossible to me."

It was a really great reminder that surrendered people are called to serve in ways that lead to joy. We don't need to fear what God will ask us to do.

Anxiety can lead us to be scared of callings, but love leads us to pursue serving in ways that fit how we were made.

Read 1 Corinthians 12:12-26.

What are we, as believers, called in this passage?

What "body part" do you think you are, or could be, in the body of Christ?

What gifts or desires has God planted in you that led you to that conclusion?

Look at verses 15-24. Have you ever wished you were a different part in the body of Christ? Have you ever been envious of someone who was called to something different?

What did that person have that you felt you were lacking? How do you think Jesus would speak into that feeling?

God didn't design us to be a people who tear each other down and pursue someone else's calling. We are to work together in unity with concern for each other.

Read John 13:34–35.

How does Jesus command us to treat one another?

What will this you-first love show the world, according to verse 35?

Christ set the ultimate example for us in this. He certainly could have wanted an easier job. Instead, He humbled Himself.

How does Philippians 2:8 tell us Jesus humbled Himself?

Jesus left the majesty of heaven and came here as an infant. He lived His life meeting the needs of others, and He died that excruciating death that brought His people life.

When we delight in the Lord, we are able to delight in how He made us. We are able to use the gifts He's given us to love and to serve, and it's there that we find joy. It's there that anxiety disappears. It's there that we stop worrying about our comfort and safety because we're too busy being blessed serving the needs of our friends.

What are some ways in which you feel God has uniquely equipped you to be able to serve the body?

In the space below, think of three people who have been "the body" to you, suffering in your suffering, rejoicing in your joys and delighting in your honor. Make an effort to reach out to them and encourage them this week.

1.

2.

3.

Who can you serve this week? What can you do? Who has God called you to love right now?

If you're feeling anxious about your calling, use the space below to pray for God to grant you clarity of purpose and joy in giving yourself to the work of His kingdom. Pray for joy and peace and pray God uses you to help others see they are loved.

DAY FOUR
SCARY PEOPLE ON MONDAY NIGHTS

Romans 15:7–13 and 2 Corinthians 3:18

When I was pregnant with my youngest, I had aversions to meat and small groups. My husband was leading our group, and I was—um—vocally opposed to pregnant participation.

"I'm keeping a baby alive! How am I supposed to also be with people on Monday nights?" I would, of course, panic about it.

In my mind, small-grouping while with child was an impossible task. It meant babysitting-arranging and long-listening and people asking for help. I spent Monday afternoons worried someone on Monday night would need my help while I was trying to give all my energy and focus to baby growing. What horror!

Yep. That's me. That's your Bible study coach.

I'll never forget the night the group brainstormed about a service project we could do together.

I wanted to be transported to another planet. *What if they voted for us to go find murderers mid-murdering and tell them about Jesus? What if they asked us to gain the trust of the mid-murdering murderers by letting them babysit my newborn?*

I pondered excuses. I dreaded Monday nights.

And then, something happened. I sat beside other Jesus followers enough nights in a row that I started to love them. They answered study questions with Bible verses they had memorized. They held my baby (who was eventually born) when my arms got tired. They brought us meals when we'd had a rough week. This group loved my fear away, and their love made me want to love them back. Then, it made me want to love the whole world.

In fact, God called us to adopt Joy while we did life alongside those people.

Read Romans 15:7–13.

What does verse 7 tell us we are to do to one another as Christ has done for us?

What did Christ become on behalf of God's truth?

What did He confirm to the fathers?

In your own life, your own church, your own local body of believers, what unique opportunities do you personally have to be a servant to the people around you?

We, as the body of Christ, are able to imitate Christ by welcoming people into our lives, by serving them, by reminding them of God's promises. We do this for each other, and, as a result, we receive blessing.

What blessings does God fill us with as we believe? (See verse 13.)

"Now may the God of hope fill you with all joy and peace as you believe so that you may overflow with hope by the power of the Holy Spirit" (v. 13). That's it, guys. Welcome one another until your worries fall away. Serve until suddenly you are filled with peace. Be in the body. Please, be in the body, so that you may overflow with hope. We have such an amazing situation together in Jesus.

During my anti-small-group season of fear, I was so anxious about what people would burden me with, but it never felt like a burden. They were just people like me who pursued service in Christ, and, as a result, they had joy and peace, and it overflowed and changed me.

My anxiety evaporated when I was plugged in with those people. I felt strong around them because they were so good at meeting my needs, and I delighted in finding ways to meet theirs. It was just a natural overflow of the joy and peace I'd been given by God, through them.

It's what we are made for.

In the pie chart below, fill in what percentage of the time you feel like you are overflowing with joy and peace and what percentage of the time you are a slave to your fears.

slave to my fears

overflowing with joy and strength

It ebbs and flows. But I believe our pie charts will look different in ten years. I believe that 2 Corinthians 3:18 is true.

We all, with unveiled faces, are looking as in a mirror at the glory of the Lord and are being transformed into the same image from glory to glory; this is from the Lord who is the Spirit.

God is always transforming His children, and He often uses His other children to do it. What a gift. What a joy. We get to be part of the healing and hope and freedom of our friends.

A big contributor to anxiety is isolation. If you've been actively pushing people away from your pain, what can you do this week to bring people in?

Name another believer you can reach out to for prayer and support and help.

If you're not currently struggling, who can you support this week? Who can you encourage and support and remind that they are loved and that they are not alone?

DAY FIVE
A BALLET STUDIO, A BIOPSY, AND A BRAVE MOM

2 Corinthians 1:3—7

My mom and I were in the bathroom at my daughter's ballet studio when she told me she'd found a lump. It took my breath away. Cancer? The very worst of the bad, scary things? My mom?

It was a surreal year. She had surgery. She had chemo. She had radiation. She went bald. She was living out my worst nightmare.

The first time I went to go see her during her chemo treatment, I was struck by my surroundings. She was at the end of a long, white, sterile hallway. In every room I passed, I saw bald women with sad faces and tired faces and scared faces.

All I could think was, *This is the valley of the shadow of death.*

And then I got to my mom's room, and there she was. Curly rainbow-colored wig. Venti Frappuccino®. Her laptop on the table and her big Bible in her lap.

"My baby!" she chirped.

There she was, at the end of the valley, showing me how to walk through it. My mom was being comforted by the Word of God, and she was able to comfort me with her testimony.

Years later, when I walked through a cancer scare, I thought of her and her faith and her peace. I remembered the hope we share in Jesus, and the surgeries and the waiting weren't as scary.

Read 2 Corinthians 1:3-7.

Anyone would agree that the cancer patient who is currently having red poison infused into her bloodstream is the one who needs comfort. But, through the power of Christ, God is able to use the afflicted to reveal His power. The power He has gives us peace when life is the opposite of peaceful.

What did Paul call God in verse 3?

Commentator David E. Garland said, "Here he identifies him as the Father of all mercies and God of all comfort and implies that mercies and comfort are brought to realization through Christ."[2]

This is important because through Christ, God is able to comfort us since Christ defeated sin and death. Christ broke the curse so that all this broken-sad-scariness we live with will one day be gone. God can comfort us because He is the only One with the power to comfort us. His comfort isn't false or temporary. It's powerful. It's eternal. It's shareable.

According to verse 4, what are we able to do with the comfort God gives us in our affliction?

Verses 4-5 tells us the comfort of Christ overflows out of us as believers. A Christian comforting another Christian isn't just a "there, there" with a pat on the back. A Christian is a Spirit-filled messenger, sharing tears and sharing hope that one day, as Sally Lloyd-Jones put it, "everything sad will come untrue."[3]

What are some ways other believers have comforted you when you were feeling anxious or afflicted?

You can't be convinced the world is caving in while being convinced that the world is being made new. Anxiety is complicated. And there are so many reasons for it and so many biological and emotional factors. But when we bring our fears and our doubts into the light, when we do life alongside other believers, we see that though they walk through scary things, like cancer, they also walk with hope and comfort. That stuff is contagious. The hope, not the cancer. Praise God.

My mom's peace poured out in that infusion clinic when she was having her cancer treatments. It touched me, and it touched nurses, and it touched doctors, and it touched other people suffering the same sickness.

Her joy made people think, *Why? What is this hope? Where is this comfort coming from?*

In the space below, ask God to comfort you in the areas of your life that trigger anxiety. Ask Him to use that comfort not just to remind you of your soul's safety and hope, but to spill onto others who are anxious too.

Alone, we're anxious. Alone, we're convinced this world is going to eat us alive. But together, we're walking reminders, we're walking proof, that though Jesus was right when He said, "In this world you will have trouble" (John 16:33, NIV), He was also right when He said we can "take heart!" because He has overcome the world.

I wish I had the words and the power to end this study promising you that completing this book would help you overcome anxiety. I can't make that promise though. I'm powerless; I'm sinful; and I'm so often scared too. But I know God made us to bring Him glory. I know He is glorified when anxious people remind other anxious people of the truth. The truth that raises dead people to life and gives hopeless people hope. This truth that is so powerful, it changes us from self-centered, isolated, insulated people into joy-filled, purpose-driven, ambassadors of peace. We live in a scary place, and we are weak. But that's not all. We are held together by a Savior who has won and is winning and will win forever over every anxious thing.

Cling to His Word. Cling to this thrilling hope. Cling to others who are held together by Him and rejoice with me that we are loved, that we are free, that we are safe in all the ways that matter most, and that one day we'll be safe forever.

NOTES

This past week, you completed the Session Eight personal study in your books. If you weren't able to do so, no big deal! You can still follow along with the questions, be involved in the discussion, and watch the video. When you are ready to begin, open up your time in prayer and push play on Video Eight for Session Eight.

WATCH

Write down any thoughts, verses, or things you want to remember as you watch the video for Session Eight of Anxious.

REVIEW SESSION EIGHT PERSONAL STUDY

From Day One: Have you ever experienced a season of discouragement? What were the circumstances, and what were you feeling?

From Day Two: According to Acts 2:42-47, what were the early Christians devoted to? How do these things compare to what you or the believers in your life are devoted to?

From Day Three: Have you ever wished you were a different part in the body of Christ? Have you ever been envious of someone who was called to something different?

From Day Four: What does Romans 15:7 tell us we are to do to one another as Christ has done for us?

From Day Five: According to 2 Corinthians 1:4, what are we able to do with the comfort God gives us in our affliction? What are some ways other believers have comforted you when you were feeling anxious or afflicted?

FROM THIS WEEK'S STUDY

As a group, review this week's memory verse.

And let us consider one another in order to provoke love and good works, not neglecting to gather together, as some are in the habit of doing, but encouraging each other, and all the more as you see the day approaching.

HEBREWS 10:24-25

DISCUSS

This week, we looked at how God created us for community. He created us to comfort and encourage each other. He created us to hold each other together in this often scary and unpredictable life. Allow time for anyone who wants to share a testimony of God comforting them in a way that comforted others or of them being comforted by God through others.

Do you tend to isolate or seek community when you feel anxious? If you isolate, who will you ask to hold you accountable, to reach out, to make sure you're not trying to fight alone when you're struggling?

Reflect on what God has taught you about fighting anxiety throughout this week. What have you learned that helped you the most? Which Scriptures have been most comforting? What will you do differently going forward as you fight the good fight and finish the race (2 Tim. 4:7)?

PRAY

Close out your time together in prayer, thanking God for what He's done, thanking Him for being our source of comfort and hope in a world full of scary things. Lift up the specific requests of your group members to the Lord in faith, believing He is sovereign and working all things together for the good of those who love Him and are called according to His purpose (Rom. 8:28).

To access the teaching sessions, use the instructions in the back of your Bible study book.

Appendix

BECOMING A CHRISTIAN

Romans 10:17 says, "So faith comes from what is heard, and what is heard comes through the message about Christ."

Maybe you've stumbled across new information in this study. Maybe you've attended church all your life, but something you read here struck you differently than it ever has before. Or maybe you are exhausted from wrestling with anxiety, and you are looking for the rest and peace that can only come from casting your cares on Jesus, who cares for you. If you have never accepted Christ but would like to, read on to discover how you can become a Christian.

Your heart tends to run from God and rebel against Him. The Bible calls this sin. Romans 3:23 says, "For all have sinned and fall short of the glory of God."

Yet God loves you and wants to save you from sin, to offer you a new life of hope. John 10:10b says, "I have come so that they may have life and have it in abundance."

To give you this gift of salvation, God made a way through His Son, Jesus Christ. Romans 5:8 says, "But God proves his own love for us in that while we were still sinners, Christ died for us."

You receive this gift by faith alone. Ephesians 2:8-9 says, "For you are saved by grace through faith, and this is not from yourselves; it is God's gift—not from works, so that no one can boast."

Faith is a decision of your heart demonstrated by the actions of your life. Romans 10:9 says, "If you confess with your mouth, 'Jesus is Lord,' and believe in your heart that God raised him from the dead, you will be saved."

If you trust that Jesus died for your sins and want to receive new life through Him, pray a prayer similar to the following one to express your repentance and faith in Him.

Dear God, I know I am a sinner. I believe Jesus died to forgive me of my sins. I accept Your offer of eternal life. Thank You for forgiving me of all my sins. Thank You for my new life. From this day forward, I will choose to follow You.

If you have trusted Jesus for salvation, please share your decision with your group leader or another Christian friend. If you are not already attending church, find one in which you can worship and grow in your faith. Following Christ's example, ask to be baptized as a public expression of your faith.

SCARLET'S FAVORITE
FEAR-FIGHTING VERSES

Put these in your pocket. Tape them to your mirrors. Write them on your childrens' faces! This is truth. These words have power. This is how we fight.

Be strong and courageous. Do not fear or be in dread of them, for it is the LORD your God who goes with you. He will not leave you or forsake you.
DEUTERONOMY 31:6 (ESV)

Have I not commanded you? Be strong and courageous. Do not be frightened, and do not be dismayed, for the LORD your God is with you wherever you go.
JOSHUA 1:9 (ESV)

I sought the LORD, and he answered me and delivered me from all my fears.
PSALM 34:4 (ESV)

When I am afraid, I put my trust in you.
PSALM 56:3 (ESV)

You will keep the mind that is dependent on you in perfect peace, for it is trusting in you.
ISAIAH 26:3

Fear not, for I am with you; be not dismayed, for I am your God; I will strengthen you, I will help you, I will uphold you with my righteous right hand.
ISAIAH 41:10 (ESV)

Therefore I tell you, do not be anxious about your life, what you will eat or what you will drink, nor about your body, what you will put on. Is not life more than food, and the body more than

clothing? Look at the birds of the air: they neither sow nor reap nor gather into barns, and yet your heavenly Father feeds them. Are you not of more value than they? And which of you by being anxious can add a single hour to his span of life? And why are you anxious about clothing? Consider the lilies of the field, how they grow: they neither toil nor spin, yet I tell you, even Solomon in all his glory was not arrayed like one of these.
MATTHEW 6:25-29 (ESV)

Therefore, since we have been justified by faith, we have peace with God through our Lord Jesus Christ. Through him we have also obtained access by faith into this grace in which we stand, and we rejoice in hope of the glory of God. Not only that, but we rejoice in our sufferings, knowing that suffering produces endurance, and endurance produces character, and character produces hope, and hope does not put us to shame, because God's love has been poured into our hearts through the Holy Spirit who has been given to us. For while we were still weak, at the right time Christ died for the ungodly.
ROMANS 5:1-6 (ESV)

For our sake he made him to be sin who knew no sin, so that in him we might become the righteousness of God.
2 CORINTHIANS 5:21 (ESV)

Do not be anxious about anything, but in everything by prayer and supplication with thanksgiving let your requests be made known to God. And the peace of God, which surpasses all understanding, will guard your hearts and your minds in Christ Jesus.
PHILIPPIANS 4:6-7 (ESV)

For God gave us a spirit not of fear but of power and love and self-control.
2 TIMOTHY 1:7 (ESV)

There is no fear in love; instead, perfect love drives out fear . . .
1 JOHN 4:18a

ENDNOTES

SESSION ONE

1. Snacks are not required but strongly recommended.

2. Tim Keller, "The Wounded Spirit," *Gospel in Life*, December 5, 2004, accessed February 18, 2021, https://gospelinlife.com/downloads/the-wounded-spirit-5389/.

SESSION TWO

1. Bible scholars say that Abimelech was sometimes used as a proper name but was also a common title for a Philistine king. So, as explained in the *Holman Illustrated Bible Dictionary* (p. 9), Abimelech may have been King Achish's title. It is likely they are the same dude.

2. C. H. Spurgeon, "Psalm XXVII" and "Psalm LII," *The Treasury of David*, Vol. II (New York: Funk & Wagnalls, 1885).

3. Ibid.

4. "Jehovah Rapha (The Lord Who Heals)," *Blue Letter Bible*, accessed February 23, 2021, https://www.blueletterbible.org/study/misc/name_god.cfm.

5. Strong's H6960, *Blue Letter Bible*, accessed February 22, 2021, https://www.blueletterbible.org/lang/lexicon/lexicon.cfm?Strongs=H6960&t=CSB.

6. *Holman Old Testament Commentary: Psalms 1–75*, Steven J. Lawson, ed. (Nashville: Broadman & Holman Publishers, 2003).

7. C. H. Spurgeon, "Psalm 61," *Treasury of David, Blue Letter Bible*, accessed February 22, 2021, via https://www.blueletterbible.org/Comm/spurgeon_charles/tod/ps061.cfm?a=539001.

8. Matthew Henry, "Commentary on Psalms 61," *Blue Letter Bible*, accessed on February 22, 2021, via https://www.blueletterbible.org/Comm/mhc/Psa/Psa_061.cfm?a=539001.

9. Ibid, *Holman Old Testament Commentary: Psalms 1–75.*

10. Elisabeth Elliot, "The Lord is My Shepherd," Series: *Elisabeth Elliot Speaks About*, accessed February 22, 2021, https://www.blueletterbible.org/audio_video/elliot_elisabeth/misc/Elisabeth_Elliot_Speaks_About.cfm#The_Lord_Is_My_Shepherd.

SESSION THREE

1. Joshua J. Mark, "Assyrian Warfare," *World History Encyclopedia*, May 2, 2018, accessed February 25, 2021, https://www.ancient.eu/Assyrian_Warfare/.

2. James Bruckner, *The NIV Application Commentary* (Grand Rapids, MI: Zondervan, 2004).

3. James Montgomery Boice, *The Minor Prophets, Vol. I* (Grand Rapids, MI: Baker Books, 1983.

4. James Montgomery Boice, *About The Minor Prophets (Hosea–Jonah): An Expositional Commentary, Vol. I* (Grand Rapids, MI: Baker Books, 2002).

5. Frank Gardner, "Iraq's Christians 'close to extinction,'" *BBC*, May 23, 2019, accessed March 1, 2021, https://www.bbc.com/news/world-middle-east-48333923.

6. Helen Howarth Lemmel, "Turn Your Eyes Upon Jesus," 1922, accessed March 1, 2021, https://hymnary.org/text/o_soul_are_you_weary_and_troubled.

7. Priscilla Shirer, *Jonah: Navigating a Life Interrupted*, video (Nashville, TN: Lifeway Christian Resources, 2010), https://www.youtube.com/watch?v=-Vb19mJcb48.

8. Note on Matthew 6:25, *ESV Study Bible* (Wheaton, IL: Crossway, 2008).

SESSION FOUR

1. Douglas K. Stuart, *The New American Commentary: Exodus, Vol. II* (Nashville: B&H Publishing Group, 2006), 113–114.

2. John Piper, "I Am Who I Am," *desiringGod*, September 16, 1984, accessed March 3, 2021, https://www.desiringgod.org/messages/i-am-who-i-am.

3. A. W. Tozer, *Knowledge of the Holy* (New York: HarperCollins, 1961), 1.

4. Charles Spurgeon, *God Always Cares* (Shawnee, KS: Gideon House Books, 2017), 33.

5. Ibid.

SESSION FIVE

1. Karen H. Jobes, *The NIV Application Commentary* (Grand Rapids, MI: Zondervan, 1999), 19–21.

2. Some translations actually say hanged (CSB, ESV, KJV) and others (NIV, NLT) say *impaled*.

3. Paul Tripp, "018. Esther Summary," *Paul Tripp Ministries: The Gospel One Chapter At a Time*, September 2, 2019, accessed March 8, 2021, https://www.paultripp.com/bible-study/posts/esther-summary.

SESSION SIX

1. Stanton W. Gavitt, "I'm So Happy And Here's the Reason Why," Singspiration Inc., 1936.

2. Strong's G5011, *Blue Letter Bible*, accessed March 30, 2021, https://www.blueletterbible.org/lang/lexicon/lexicon.cfm?Strongs=G5011&t=CSB.

3. Strong's G5013, *Blue Letter Bible*, accessed March 11, 2021, https://www.blueletterbible.org/lang/lexicon/lexicon.cfm?Strongs=G5013&t=CSB.

4. Gavitt, "I'm So Happy And Here's the Reason Why."

5. John Cotton, *The New-England Primer* (Aledo, TX: WallBuilder Press, 1991, reprint, originally pub. 1777).

SESSION SEVEN

1. Don Stewart, "What Is General Revelation," *Blue Letter Bible*, accessed March 17, 2021, https://www.blueletterbible.org/faq/don_stewart/don_stewart_370.cfm.

2. Don Stewart, "What Is Special Revelation," *Blue Letter Bible*, accessed March 17, 2021, https://www.blueletterbible.org/faq/don_stewart/don_stewart_1196.cfm.

3. Jen Wilkin, "Q&A: Applying," Instagram story, September 2020, accessed March 17, 2021, https://www.instagram.com/jenwilkin/?hl=en.

4. James Montgomery Boice, *The Gospel of John: The Coming of the Light (John 1–4)*, Vol. I, (Grand Rapids, MI: Baker Bookos, 1985,1989).

SESSION EIGHT

1. Ajith Fernando, *The NIV Application Commentary: Acts* (Grand Rapids, MI: Zondervan, 1998), 125.

2. David E. Garland, *The New American Commentary: 2 Corinthians*, Vol. 29 (Nashville: B&H Publishing Group, 1999), 59.

3. Sally Lloyd-Jones and Sam Shammas, *The Jesus Storybook Bible Curriculum*, 2011, https://www.sallylloyd-jones.com/wp-content/uploads/2014/02/jesus_storybook_bible_currkit_ot_NoMoreTears.compressed.pdf.

LET'S BE FRIENDS!

BLOG

We're here to help you grow in your faith, develop as a leader, and find encouragement as you go.

lifewaywomen.com

NEWSLETTER

Be the first to hear about new studies, events, giveaways, and more by signing up.

lifeway.com/womensnews

SOCIAL

Find inspiration in the in-between moments of life.

@lifewaywomen

APP

Download the Lifeway Women app for Bible study plans, online study groups, a prayer wall, and more!

 Google Play App Store

Lifeway.women

MORE FROM SCARLET

AVAILABLE WHERE BOOKS ARE SOLD

Get the most from your study.

Customize your Bible study time with a guided experience.

In this 8-session study with Scarlet Hiltibidal, learn that when we trust the Lord rather than fearing the brokenness in our world, we are able to take hold of the perfect peace that is only available in Him.

In this study you'll:

- Learn how to fight your anxiety with the Word of God so you can take hold of the abundant life Jesus has purchased for you.

- Realize you're not alone in your struggle with anxiety by prioritizing community and confession over isolation.

- Practice bringing your anxieties to God and come to know prayer as a pathway to peace.

Video Access (included in this Bible study book)

- Promo (1:38)
- Session One: Introduction—Anxious to Be Here (10:05)
- Session Two: Anxious David (10:04)
- Session Three: Anxious Jonah (8:45)
- Session Four: Anxious Moses (5:54)
- Session Five: Anxious Esther (9:21)
- Session Six: Anxious Prayer (6:34)
- Session Seven: Anxious Reader (7:36)
- Session Eight: Anxious Together (7:29)

ADDITIONAL RESOURCES

Visit **lifeway.com/anxious** to explore the entire study family—Bible study book with video access, eBook with video access, and teen girls' Bible study—along with a free session sample, video clips, and church promotional material.

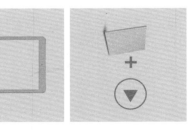